HOW TO LIVE IN A CAR, VAN, OR RV

—

And Get Out of Debt, Travel, and Find True Freedom

By Bob Wells,

A 10 Year Vandweller and Owner of cheaprvliving.com

DISCLAIMER:

Everything I am suggesting in this book is inherently riskier than living the *"normal"* American life. If you follow my advice, the possibility of your being hurt or running into trouble will dramatically increase.

If you don't want to live a riskier life, return this book to Amazon right now!

If you keep this book, and follow my advice, you are choosing a life of adventure over a life of safety, security and comfort. You are taking your life into your own hands and living life on your own terms.

I applaud you for your courage, but you must understand that you alone are responsible for the results of your choices and actions and I bear no responsibility for them at all.

Ask the average American what they think of the idea of living in a car, van or RV, and most likely they will look at you like you've lost your mind. To them such an idea is ridiculous beyond words. And yet here you are, you bought a book on how to live in a vehicle. Why would you, or anyone else, want to do such a ridiculous thing? Generally, there are two common reasons:

1) Circumstances such as a divorce, medical problems, loss of a job, or a bad economy force you into it against your will.

2) You have a compelling desire to break out of the societal norm and live a life of simplicity, freedom and travel.

If you are reading this because of reason number one, you bought the right book. Like you, I was forced into living in a van because I couldn't afford to live any other way. Having done it for over 10 years I've encountered just about every possible problem you are likely to encounter, and I'm here to offer you solutions to them. I'm writing this book to make your life as a vehicle dweller more comfortable and pleasant so that you don't merely survive your economic hardship, you thrive during it. Who knows, you may even end up liking it. Fortunately, if you bought this book because of reason number two, and the "American Dream" has become a nightmare for you, it is equally right for you.

I had never admitted to myself just how unhappy I was with living a "normal" life. But a funny thing happened soon after a bitter divorce forced me to move into a van: I started to feel happy. It didn't make any sense, I should have been miserable living in a van, but I wasn't. Just the opposite, for the first time I was truly content and at peace. It was like a giant weight had been lifted off my back. If you have come to the point where you just can't stand living in the "Rat Race" any more, vandwelling may be perfect for you.

MY STORY:

In the spring of 1995 I was going through a difficult divorce. My finances were stretched so thin I could no longer afford to live in an apartment; there just wasn't enough money to pay rent. On my way to work every day I drove past a parking lot that had a box van with a "For Sale" sign on it. One day I was on my way home worrying about my finances and the idea popped into my head, "Why don't I buy that van and move into it?" The idea struck me as crazy, but I didn't really have any alternative, I was pretty close to being homeless, so I pulled in to look at the van. It was a contractors box van and they said it ran great but it was so ratty looking (which it was) that it embarrassed the boss, so they were selling it cheap. I went to the bank right then, and took out the last of my savings, $1,500. That night I gave notice to my landlord that I was moving out and threw a sleeping pad down on the floor of the van, laid out some blankets, and officially became a "vandweller."

I won't kid you; those first few weeks of living in the van were not pleasant. The turmoil of the divorce already had me in an emotional uproar and on top of that I was "reduced" to living in a van. Many nights I cried myself to sleep. But over a period of time as I made the van more comfortable and got used to it, I started to fall in love with being a vandweller.

At the first of each month, when the rent used to be due, I really loved living in my van because that money went in my pocket! In fact even after my finances recovered from the divorce, I chose to keep living in it. I lived in that box van for the next six years. In 2002 I re-married and moved into my new wife's house. Then something very unexpected happened, I tremen-dously missed living in the van and hated living in the house.

It was a great house in a beautiful area but on the first of every month we had this huge house payment due. Plus the utility bills kept coming in and going up. Worst of all, it required constant work. The lawn had to be mowed, the snow had to be shoveled, and the toilets had to be fixed. The one thing you would think I would love about the house was all the extra room, but I hated that most of all. It was such a huge waste of space. All that space had to be dusted, vacu-umed and cleaned constantly. Even worse, it had to be heated in the winter and cooled in the summer. It seemed like we were constantly looking at new furni-ture and trinkets to fill the space. I missed the econ-omy, simplicity and freedom of my little box van.

In 2008 I finally admitted to myself that I simply could not be happy living in a house, so I divorced for the second time and moved back into a vehicle. This time I lived in a Ford F150 pickup with a home-built camper on it. As of this writing (2012) I am liv-ing in a converted cargo trailer I pull with my F150.

It isn't possible for me to be any happier! I work as a campground host in the National Forests in the summer (either the Rockies or Sierra mountains), and take the winter off by drawing unemployment and living for free on BLM desert land (generally Arizona or Nevada). By getting out of the city and reconnecting with nature, I have found a new joy and peace of mind like I had never known before. I owe all that to living in a vehicle.

WHAT IS A VANDWELLER?

Even though I was happy living in a van, when my family and friends heard about it, they were very worried about me. They thought I had hit rock bottom and become "homeless." Technically they were right, since I didn't have a traditional home I was, in fact, homeless. But I didn't think of myself or feel, homeless, I just felt happy!

The homeless face quite a stigma in our country. It is assumed they are all bums or beggars who are either mentally ill, hopeless alcoholics or drug addicts. I tried to explain to my family that while I had been forced into living in a van, I had since fallen in love with it and was now doing it by choice. Some understood and some didn't. I found it very helpful if I used terms they could understand to clarify my position. I started correcting them when they said I was homeless, and explained that I was a vandweller instead. It's important that we explore the definition of a vandweller so you can come to a better understanding of what you might be doing.

There is a continuum of people who live in their vehicles: on one end are people who are forced into living in their car, are totally broke, and have no idea where their next meal is coming from. On the other extreme end are retired people who live full-time in million dollar motor homes and stay in upscale RV parks with their own private lake and golf course. In between there are people in every possible economic situation (rich to poor) and living in everything from a 1978 Honda Civic to a huge and expensive RV.

The difference between them isn't their yearly income or value of their vehicle; it's their attitude toward living in a vehicle. Let's explore that:

HOMELESS:
The dominate attitude of the homeless toward living in a vehicle, is that they hate it. They don't want to be there and given a chance they would move back into a house as quickly as they possibly

could. It isn't an adventure, it is misery. If you are being forced to live in a vehicle, chances are very good this describes your attitude.

VANDWELLER:

A vandweller may be living in the exact same type of vehicle as the homeless guy and have the same economic situation, (or he may work at a good-paying job and live in a very nice van or RV) but the vandweller wants to be there. To him it may be unpleasant right now, but it is an adventure that he is glad he is having. He has made a deliberate choice to drop-out of the rat race and live a life of simplicity, freedom and adventure.

I think those three words are the defining terms to vandwelling: (A) Voluntary Simplicity: when you choose to live in a vehicle, you just can't have as much stuff as when you lived in a house, so you are forced into a simple life. At first it is unnatural (and probably unpleasant) but soon it will start to seem normal and natural. (B) Freedom: when you live in a vehicle you have a lot more choices. For example, if you don't like your neighbor, you just turn the key and drive away. If it's too hot or cold where you are, you can just drive to somewhere more to your liking. Now that's freedom! (C) Adventure: Living in a vehicle is inherently more dangerous and risky than living in a house so it can easily become an adventure.

A FULL-TIME RVER:

An RVer is generally (but by no means always) an older retired person who has traded his stick-and-brick home for an RV, but their life doesn't really change that much. When someone moves out of a house and into an RV, they are embracing a great deal more simplicity, freedom and adventure than they ever had before, so in that way they are like vandwellers. However, I think it is a matter of degrees. Most RVers lives don't change that drastically when they move out of their house. In many ways it's just like it was before. Most of them can't relate to the extreme simplicity, freedom and adventure that most vandwellers crave. Generally, the ones I've talked to just couldn't understand how I could live in such a crude way in such a tiny space. There was as big a gulf between us as there is between me and most traditional house dwellers.

On the other hand, I've known some seemingly very traditional RVers who fit in extremely well at a gathering of vandwellers. I'm pretty sure if some of them were 40 years younger, they would have been there in a bare-bones van looking for their next big adventure. In their hearts they had the same attitude, even if their lives weren't as simple, free or adventurous as ours, so we could embrace them as fellow vandwellers.

Vandwellers are Rule-Breakers: There is one common denominator to all the vandwellers I have ever met. They are all rule-breakers. I'm not talking about being outlaws or criminals. That is a totally different thing that involves a disregard for other people, and I almost never see that in vandwellers. Almost universally we are polite and considerate. The idea of stealing from or harming others is unthinkable. No, we are rule-breakers in the sense that we make a deliberate decision to NOT live by societies unwritten rules:

1-Get a job and work it 5 days a week
   until you are old and worn-out. Only
   then can you relax and enjoy life.

2-Buy a house. Then sell it and buy
   a bigger house... repeat.

3-Buy lots of stuff. When something better
   comes out, buy it. Never stop buying!

These rules work extremely well to make our society and economic system function like a well-oiled machine. The problem is, we are people and not machines so we become unhappy drones whose well-being is completely unimportant as long as the machine functions well.

Every vandweller I know has rejected those rules and is marching to the beat of a different drummer. We live on the outskirts of the law and it is so upsetting to society that many communities have passed laws to make what we do illegal. For example, if we are caught sleeping on the street in a van we can be fined or even imprisoned. At the minimum we will be given the 'bums-rush" and asked to move on.

A homeless person may live in a van, but he isn't there because he hates society's rules. No, he has one goal and that is to get back under the tyranny of those rules where he feels comfortable and safe. The great majority of RVers have spent their whole life obeying society's rules and in their old age they are going to bend them a little. But in their hearts they aren't non-conformists.

Vandwelling is ultimately a rejection of society's traditional, unwritten rules and a choice to live life in a way that makes you happy.

A LIFE WITH NO REGRETS:

"Twenty years from now you will be more disappointed by the things that you didn't do than by the ones you did do—So throw off the bowlines.— Sail away from the safe harbor — Catch the trade winds in your sails —Explore. Dream. Discover."

—Mark Twain

When I look back at my life, being forced to live in a van was one of the very best things that ever happened to me (the only thing better was the birth of my children.) Before then I had spent my whole life doing what I was told. I got married, got a job, and had kids. Week after week, year after year, decade after decade, I went to a job I hated, worked with people I didn't like, in order to buy things I didn't want. I was the living embodiment of Thoreau's quote that most men lived lives of quiet desperation. I went to work, came home tired, ate dinner, watched TV and then did it again the next day. I lived for my free time on the weekends but there was no free time. There were always things that had to be done around the house and errands that had to be run. On the few weeks I got off a year we went on vacation and tried to cram a years' worth of fun into those few days. My life was a boring, drab routine of doing what I was told I was supposed to do.

I knew I was not happy, but it never occurred to me that I could be, it just wasn't an option. Then came the divorce. Up till then my life hadn't been happy, but at least it wasn't bad, it was acceptable. For a long time after the divorce my life was really bad, but after I moved into the van, everything started to change. I had extra money so I started working only 32 hours a week. Every weekend was a three day weekend, which allowed me to spend more time with my kids and tremendously helped my mental outlook on life. As soon as I could, I took early retirement and now live in my camper.

Today I only work for 6 months a year as a campground host in the summer and live for free in the desert in the winter. I like my job, I like the people I work with, and I only buy the things that I really want. At last, I am truly happy.

You've got a lot of choices. If getting out of bed in the morning is a chore and you're not smiling on a regular basis, try another choice.

—Steven D. Woodhull

Are you smiling on a regular basis? Are you happy or are you just going through the motions that society requires of you. Answer these questions honestly:

- Are you happy, or are you just treading water, only enduring life?

- Is your life full of joy, or is it full of stress?

- Do you love your job and wake up wanting to get to work, or is it a drudgery?

- Are you sick of the constant competition at work, in traffic, and even for parking spaces?

- Do you ever look around your house and say, "Where did all this stuff come from, why do I have it? I feel like I am in prison." And yet you keep going to the store to buy even more.

- Do you like fighting traffic, breathing bad air, spending fifty weeks a year looking forward to two weeks of happiness? When those two weeks come, do they just fly by, leaving you no more happy than you were before?

If you don't like your answers, maybe it's time to make a different choice. Unfortunately, for most people, **an acceptable present is better than an unknown and risky future**. The reason is very simple, fear holds them back. Being afraid is reasonable; living in a vehicle is so unconventional it seems very risky. But, when all the problems are addressed in a simple, straightforward way, you will see that the risks are very minor.

In fact the single greatest risk most of us will face is that when we come to the end of our lives we will look back and see that we never really lived at all. I believe that is one of the greatest tragedies that can befall a human being. I pray that doesn't happen to you. To help you overcome your fear, let's look at the wonderful rewards that make vehicle living worth any risk:

TEN REASONS YOU SHOULD LIVE IN A VAN:

The proper function of man is to live, not to exist. – I shall not waste my days in trying to prolong them.

—Jack London

1) You can survive hard times: For most of us money is our single greatest fear. In this section I want to show you that no matter what happens to you (if you are going through a divorce, been laid off from work, or simply don't make enough money to live on) living in a van will not only let you survive, it will help you thrive. I look at it this way, living in a van means you will never be homeless, you will always have a roof over your head. And in these bad economic times, that has become very important.

No matter how tight your budget is right now, not having to pay for rent or a mortgage payment (along with the utilities that go along with them) has to be a huge help financially. But what if that isn't enough? What if you still don't have enough money to live on?

After having a roof over your head, your next highest survival priority is finding food to eat. Fortunately, no matter how little money you have, getting food is easy. In nearly every major city there are many ways to get food for free.

All states have a food stamp program and you should find out if you qualify for it. Most larger towns have Rescue Missions or Soup Kitchens that hand out meals for people in need, and Food Banks that hand out canned goods and other foods. And (while it might sound gross) you can eat remarkably well by dumpster diving. That means jumping into the dumpsters behind bakeries, restaurants and grocery stores and digging around for safe, edible food. Between all those resources, you should be able to eat for free.

So your two biggest expenses (food and shelter) can be free to you if you live in a van. That should reduce your need for money to next to nothing. However, you will still need some money for:

- gas,
- repairs
- insurance for your car,
- your cell phone and internet access,
- entertainment
- and miscellaneous expenses

Where will that little bit of money come from? The obvious answer is to get a job, but as I write this in 2012, the unemployment rate has remained very high for several years. In fact many people have been unemployed for so long, they have given up hope of ever getting a job. If you follow my advice, you will have reduced your living expenses so much you should be able to make enough to live on by working part time in unconventional jobs such as:

- temp work,

- day laborer,

- as a clerk at a fast food restaurant
or convenience store

- farm labor

- selling on eBay.com

- making and selling arts and crafts

Even if you can't find a job, you can probably get the small amount of money you need by working for yourself. Here is one simple example: buy a used $50 lawn mower and a snow shovel, and you can make enough to live on just going door to door mowing lawns in the summer and shoveling driveways in the winter. I just throw that out as an example, maybe that idea won't work for you, but if you are creative, you can probably think of one that will.

The point is that by living in a van, and eating for free, you can survive any situation that life might throw at you.

2) You can get out of debt. The average American is very deeply in debt, especially credit card debt. Credit card debt is a horrible prison because once you reach a certain amount; just paying the minimum monthly payments only pays the interest, not the principle. So even if you have a job and are paying all your bills every month, you will never pay it off and get out of debt.

But moving out of a house or an apartment and into a van will allow you to pay it off fairly quickly. For example, let's say you are paying $500 a month for a small apartment and you move out of it and into a van. You take that $500 a month and instead of giving it to the person who is the LORD of your life (landlord) you put all of it towards one credit card. At the end of the year you will have paid $6,000 toward that card. No matter how much your debt is if you keep doing that for a few years, eventually you will get out of debt.

3) Living in a van is good for your mental, physical and emotional well-being. Modern science has established beyond any doubt that stress is terribly destructive to our physical, mental and emotional health. Living in a van dramatically reduced my stress levels, and I believe it will do the same for you. Let me show you a few ways it can.

A-Get out of Debt: We just looked at a huge way to reduce your stress level by getting out of debt. Most of us have some debt, and many of us have a huge amount of debt. Wouldn't it feel wonderful if at the first of every month you didn't have to watch your paycheck disappear to your debtors? Wouldn't that greatly reduce you stress level?

B-Quit a job you hate: Chances are you work at a job you don't like because you have no choice. You need the paycheck so desperately, your employer knows he can treat you any way he wants and you can't leave. By living in a van you will need so much less money that you literally can say to him, *"Take this job and shove it!"* and find a job you actually like, even if you earn less. Not going to a job you hate every day will tremendously reduce your stress level!

C-Work less hours a week: Or you can do what I did and stop working 40 hours a week and drop down to 32 hours a week. What a difference that made in my happiness level! Every week was suddenly a 3-day holiday week. My stress levels dropped dramatically. How would your life improve if you had an extra day-off every week?

D-Enjoy your weekends: Plus, the simplicity of my life made my weekends much more pleasant. I didn't have to mow a lawn or shovel snow. There weren't any repairs to be made around the house or any payments to make. My weekends were mine to enjoy.

E-Less of a commute: I used to commute 30 miles to work through some really bad traffic. By living in a van, I was able to park a few blocks away from work and avoid the commute completely. Once I stopped commuting, I became aware of how much the stop-and-go traffic stressed me out.

F-Get physically fit: Another way living in a van improved my life was going to the gym. Since I didn't have a shower in my van, I got a gym membership and went to the gym every day to shower. Since I was already there, I started running on the treadmill and working out with the weights. I discovered I enjoyed working out and was a natural distance runner. I was a big, heavy guy, and ran very slowly, but when I started running, I could just keep running for a long time. I started running in 5k, 10k and half marathon races, and in 2002 I finished a 26.2 mile Marathon. That all happened because living in a van forced me into the gym and created the free time for me to pursue my real interests.

4) Take a Sabbatical from Work: For most of us, our house or apartment payments are our single largest monthly expense. By eliminating it we gain a lot of freedom. If you cut your monthly expenses in half, you can also work half as much; wouldn't that be wonderful! But you have another choice, you could keep working your full time job and take the money you used to pay to a landlord or a mortgage and put it in the bank instead. Then quit your job and live on your savings.

For example, let's say your apartment rent is $500 a month and you need another $500 a month to live on. After you move into your van, you keep making your apartment payment, but instead of paying the landlord you become the Lord of your life and you pay yourself by putting that money into a savings account. After a year, you will have $6,000 in savings. Since you are only spending $500 a month to live, you can now quit your job and live on your savings for a full year. Instead of working for the weekend, your whole life could be a weekend. Now that is freedom!!

Security is mostly a superstition. It does not exist in nature, nor do the children of men as a whole experience it. Avoiding danger is not safer in the long run than outright exposure. Life is either a daring adventure, or nothing.

—Helen Keller

5) Adventure: Today's society is obsessed with safety. We laughingly call it the "nanny state." Unfortunately, it isn't a joke. Every possible risk to our safety is chased down and eliminated as if we were two-year-olds who can't take care of ourselves. But genetically, our body and our minds were designed to face danger. For hundreds-of-thousands of years, as hunter-gatherers, death lurked around our every corner. Every day was an adventure!

But it isn't that way anymore. For most of us life has become boring, almost intolerable in its monotony. In an evolutionary blink of an eye, humans went from being in constant danger, to never being in real danger. It's impossible for us to adopt to that much change, in that short a period of time. I firmly believe that the most of today's societal problems can be traced back to that sudden change.

Some of us turn to drugs and alcohol for relief. Others turn to crime, sexual promiscuity, risky games and adventures so they can feel alive. Sadly, the great majority live lives of quit desperation, never feeling anything deeply. **They are the ones who, on their death beds, look back at their long, safe, boring lives and realize they never lived**.

When you choose to live in a vehicle, you open yourself up to risk. You have stepped far out of the normal Americans comfort zone. There are moments of genuine fear. For example, many times I have woke up in the middle of the night to a thump on the van and I couldn't remember exactly where I was and I didn't have a clue what was outside banging on the van. One time I accidently parked in the "wrong" part of town and woke up in the middle of the night to some homeless fellows outside drinking and screaming. A friend of mine lived in a box van and woke up in the middle of the night to a graffiti artist "tagging" his van.

Because I live on public land, I spend nearly all my time in nature and that is inherently dangerous. Four times in the last few years I have been walking in the woods and seen a black bear within 30 yards. Once I was within three feet of a rattlesnake. Dozens of times I have been within fifty yards of a pair of coyotes, a few times within 10 yards. Rarely have I been in serious danger, although once I believe I was being stalked by a mountain lion. But many times my heart has pounded and the adrenaline pumped through my body. I might be safer living in a house, but that isn't what I was made for.

If you decide to live in a van or RV, you will have many friends who will try to talk you out of it, telling you it is too risky. I'm telling you the fact that it is risky is the very reason you should do it! By returning to a life with adventure in it, you are returning to a "normal" and natural human condition.

6) Travel: There is a deep, genetic urge in most of us to travel. For hundreds-of-thousands of years humans were hunter-gatherers. Virtually every day the men would travel many miles searching for game and watching out for enemies. Exploring their area was an essential part of life for them. As the seasons changed and the game moved or became scarce, the whole tribe would move.

Because we are genetically disposed to travel, explore and see new things, don't be surprised if you have *"itchy feet,"* a constant desire to travel and see what's around the next corner. Living in a vehicle can let you scratch that itch and start traveling. Using the strategy laid out above of working until you have enough savings, then quitting your job, you can travel for as long as your savings lasts. After all, your home is on wheels, why not hit the road and explore?

There are places in this country that are so beautiful they take your breath away. Wouldn't you love to see them? Or if you are interested in art, culture or history, America has a tremendous amount of that as well. It would be a terrible shame to live here all your life and not see it. Living in a vehicle will give you the freedom to do just that.

After you have traveled for a while, your savings will start to run low. Then you'll need to stop and find a new job. One option is to return to your home and find a job there. But I think there are better choices. Why not include your work with your hobbies and interests?

Maybe you like to ski, so you plan your travels to end up in Colorado and find a job at a ski resort (skiing on the weekends) and work through the winter. When your savings build back up, you hit the road again. Or maybe you like history, you can go to Gettysburg, Colonial Williamsburg, Custer National Monument, or some other historical place and get a job for the summer. If you like entertainment you can work at Disneyland or Universal Studios for the winter. Wherever there is tourism, there is a job waiting for you and often you can make more in tips than you do in wages.

7) Getting Back to Nature: Today's houses are designed to totally separate us from nature. They are heavily insulated and weatherproofed so we don't feel hot or cold. They are soundproofed so you can't hear traffic, but that also means you can't hear the birds singing. Any element that might make you even slightly uncomfortable is kept away from you. Unfortunately, that also means we are isolated from the very things that bring us the greatest joy, like falling asleep to the sound of a burbling brook, the smell after a spring rain, the sounds of birds singing in the morning, the glory of wildflowers in full bloom, a breath-taking sunrise or sunset or the deeply moving sight of the Milky Way in all its glory.

If you are like me, and live year-around on public land, you are going to find yourself reconnecting with nature (I love to say that I may live in a tiny home, but I have an enormous backyard). But even if you live in a van in a city, you will probably still spend more time in nature.

When I lived in my box van in a city, I always found public parks to be the ideal way to pass time. I loved cooking a meal on a picnic table in the shade while people-watching. Most parks had restrooms where I could use the toilet and do a quick, subtle wash-up and fill my water bottles. Some even had pools where I could swim and then take a shower.

Beyond that, living in a vehicle makes you more a part of the natural rhythm of life. When it is hot, you are hot, when it's cold, you are cold. When it's windy the van shakes around. When the birds sing, you smile. When a raven lands on your roof, you hear the clacking of his talons. You are closer to nature even while inside your van.

I personally have found a much greater sense of inner peace by reconnecting with the natural order of things, especially while living on public land (literally in a van down by the river). Why would that be? Because I got back to my original hunter-gatherer roots and was living in harmony with my genetic background. Unfortunately many of us have so severely broken all ties with nature that we aren't even aware of the loss. But one look at the rampant problems of modern society will tell us all is not well. Most of our physical, psychological and spiritual problems could be resolved if we stopped being afraid of nature and embraced it instead.

8) Spirituality: That word may turn you off, but let me assure you I am not talking about any kind of religion or dogma but something very different. Who among us hasn't watched a beautiful sunset and been deeply moved by its beauty? Who hasn't been outside on a dark night and looked at the Milky Way and felt very small, thinking, "There must be something greater than me out there!" I believe that those moments are our true spiritual birthright and ought to occur frequently. Since I have been living in National Forest in the summer and on public desert land in the winter, those moments have become a regular part of my life. I live with a deep knowing that everything in my life is just as it ought to be.

Whatever your background, or wherever you park, moving into a van can bring you to a deeper spiritual life if you want it to. That decision is entirely yours to make.

9) Making Deep, Life-Long Friends: Paradoxically I have made more real friends since I moved into a van than I ever did while living in a house. I don't just mean co-workers or neighbors I say hello to in passing. No, I mean people I make a deep connection to and hope to spend time with every year for the rest of my life. And that is true of all the vandwellers I know. It doesn't matter if we were loners or outgoing in our old life, when we became vandwellers we suddenly found ourselves with more friends than we ever had before. And not just more friends, but deeper and more intense friendships.

I've given a lot of thought to why this would be true, and even talked to other vandwellers about it. We have come up with three reasons:

1) We have more free time to make friends.

2) We have less stress in our lives, so making friends is easier.

3) We have a common lifestyle.

I'm sure that all plays a role, but I think there is something more. I think it goes back to the fact that vandwellers live a non-traditional life outside of society's rules. This underlying non-conformity creates a bond among us that very few people experience. When I meet another vandweller there is a meeting of kindred spirits. In a sense it is an underlying, subconscious "us-against-them" spirit. We share a deep "knowing" that we have found a different, nontraditional (and we think better) way of life.

I think there is an untamed wildness deep in the heart of vandwellers, and when we meet, that wildness in me recognizes the wildness in you, and an unbreakable bond is formed. There is a historical analogy that illustrates this very well: the Mountain Men of the early 1800s. Each of them abandoned their old life of drudgery and headed off to the mountains to live a much more unpleasant and difficult life in the spectacular beauty and freedom of the mountains.

They lived predominantly solitary lives but whenever their paths crossed they had an instant connection and bond with each other. Once a year they gathered together and had a Mountain Man Fur Rendezvous which was a wild party and chance to sell their furs. Even though they were highly individualistic, the mountain men shared a common life of wild adventure and freedom that bonded them in ways that few city dwelling, flatlanders could even begin to comprehend.

In 2010 I decided to follow in the footsteps of the Mountain Men and created the Rubber Tramp Rendezvous (RTR). A yearly gathering in the winter in Quartzsite, Arizona where vandwellers could gather, make friends and celebrate our wonderful lifestyle. It has been a gigantic success. The first year we had 45 people, the second 90 of us gathered in the Arizona desert. Just like the Mountain Men before us, we instantly formed bonds of friendship that transcended anything we had every known before. And the common bond was the same as the Mountain Men; we couldn't stand living a "normal" life of monotony, boredom and drudgery, and instead chose a life of freedom even though it was harder and sometimes even unpleasant.

"Unnecessary possessions are unnecessary burdens – If you have them, you have to take care of them! –There is great freedom in simplicity of living. – It is those who have enough but not too much who are the happiest".

— Peace Pilgrim

10) Simplicity: Consumerism is the true god of modern America. Every day, in a thousand ways, we are bombarded with messages telling us how much we need product X, that without it, we will never be happy. We may claim we aren't susceptible to advertising, but the truth is we are all subtly influenced by it. It leaves us feeling empty, and believing we won't be happy until we have the latest and greatest thing. The tragedy is, that as soon as we get it, we stop caring about it, we feel just as empty as we did before and we start chasing after the next greatest thing that will finally make us happy.

The countries tremendous amount of debt, especially credit card debt, and our extremely low savings rate stand as testimony to the power of advertising. Many of us want to break free of the hold of consumerism, but we don't know how. Living in a vehicle may be the solution for you.

The tiny space of a car or van (RVs hold more, but still much less than any house) demands that you pare your life down to the absolute minimum. There simply isn't room for much "stuff." You will quickly come to the point where if something new is going to come into the van, something has to go out first. On a very regular basis I examine everything in my camper and demand that it justify the amount of space it takes up. If I'm not using it, or can't see when I will be using it, I get rid of it.

Doing this over-and-over again begins to re-program your thinking away from consumerism. Instead of seeing something and trying to justify to yourself why you have to have it, you begin to see things and try to figure out a way to do without it. Plus, you probably aren't going to have a TV, the most powerful form of advertising. Being free of the hold of consumerism is very liberating.

THE FIRST STEP: GETTING RID OF STUFF:

> *"He who would travel happily must travel light".*
>
> —Antoine de St. Exupery

Hopefully you have decided to become a vehicle dweller, so what's next? That's simple, look around your current home and imagine trying to fit all that stuff into a car, van or RV. For must of us, that is a laughable idea, no way it's all going in there. Paring your stuff down to the bare minimum may take a long time and be emotionally draining, so I suggest you get started on it right away.

First we have to decide what to do with everything that won't fit. Basically you have three choices:

(A) Give it to friends or family to store for you.

(B) Put it in a storage facility and pay the monthly fees.

(C) Get rid of it.

Everybody is different, only you can decide which of these is right for you. Let me play devil's advocate while you are deciding: unless you have lived in a vehicle before, you really don't know for a fact that you are going to like it. What if you get rid of all your sentimental treasures and sell other things for pennies on the dollar, and then a few months later you decide you hate living in a vehicle and are going to go back to a house? You will have thrown away a lot of money and lost some personal treasures. As a compromise, you might want to put your most valuable or sentimental things into storage—just in case. After a few months or a year of living in a vehicle, you will be in a better position to decide if you want to keep storing it or sell it.

> *"Everything we possess that is not necessary for life or happiness becomes a burden, and scarcely a day passes that we do not add to it".*
>
> —Robert Brault,

Having said that, it is my personal belief that simplicity of life is valuable in and of itself (whether you live in a house or a van) and that you should take this opportunity to shed as much of your excess stuff as you possibly can. That way, if you do go back to house living, you will have improved your life by the simplicity you learned living in the van.

Chances are, most of your stuff doesn't really mean anything to you, you just fell victim of our consumer driven society and bought stuff you don't really want and now it has become more a burden than a blessing. Whether you live in a house or a van, you should probably get rid of all of that stuff, and lighten your load. Only put things into storage if they are of great sentimental or practical value to you.

"Anything you cannot relinquish when it has outlived its usefulness possesses you, and in this materialistic age a great many of us are possessed by our possessions."

—Peace Pilgrim

Becoming a vehicle dweller is like giving birth to a new life, and giving birth is generally is very painful. While going through your stuff you will be faced with some very difficult decisions. There will be things you really like and want to keep but you just don't have room so you have to get rid of it. In those moments you will learn whether you own your possessions, or they own you. Are you the master or the slave of your possessions?

I consider myself lucky because I was forced into living in a van. I had no choice but get rid of everything that wouldn't fit into my box van, no matter how painful it was. Later, after I fell in love with vandwelling, I had to get rid of even more stuff when I moved into my much smaller camper. By then it was easier and less painful. I just kept reminding myself that vandwelling had brought me so much joy, happiness and peace of mind, it was worth whatever sacrifice I had to make to continue doing it. That made it easy. I just looked at my stuff and said to myself, "I have finally found happiness, am I willing to trade it for this thing?" That brought things into perspective. I highly recommend this question to you as you go through your house:

"I am finally starting to follow my dream, am I willing to throw it away for this thing?"

Even with your dream in mind, it will be difficult to let go of some things, those are the ones you put into storage until you are certain you love vehicle living.

AN EXERCISE IN FREEDOM:

"Have nothing in your houses that you do not know to be useful or believe to be beautiful."

—William Morris

Getting rid of your stuff is going to take some time, so get started right now. I mean that literally. Turn off your Kindle or shut the lid on your laptop and go get some boxes or grocery sacks. Whatever room you are in look around and collect everything that is not useful or beautiful and put it into the sacks. Then come back, start the computer and continue reading.....

"Anything you cannot relinquish, when it has outlived its usefulness, possesses you, and in this materialistic age a great many of us are possessed by our possessions".

—Peace Pilgrim

If you collected everything that was not useful, you probably collected a lot of stuff! There may have been very little left. Did you find it difficult to contemplate getting rid of all that stuff? Did you feel lost and depressed at the thought of being stripped of your precious things? Did something deep down inside you scream out that you must not do this?

"In our rich consumers' civilization – we spin cocoons around ourselves – and get possessed by our possessions."

—Max Lerner

Unfortunately, our very identity becomes wrapped up in our things. They define and comfort us. They are our cocoon, giving us a sense of safety. They separate us from the danger that lurks all around us, giving us comfort from our many fears. Long ago we hid behind thick walls and a moat, today we hide behind layers of trinkets. For much of our lives all that stuff made us feel safe, but now it has become a prison. It is the master, and we are the slaves.

"It is preoccupation with possessions,— more than anything else – that prevents us from living freely and nobly.

—Bertrand Russell

Living out of a vehicle means living life at its most basic and simple level so that we can find the maximum freedom. First and foremost, that means freedom from the tyranny of our possessions. The battle lines are drawn, and they are plastic sacks full of the things that were once our best friends, but have now become our mortal enemies. If we are to live freely and nobly, we must die to them and they must go away. It's the moment of decision. What will you do? **Will you choose the safety and comfort of your pleasant prison of pretty possessions, or will you grab a free life full of chance and risk and beauty and joy?** Now is the time to get rid of all those sacks full of poison.

Here are my suggestions on how to get rid of your stuff:

(A) Sell it on craiglist or eBay.com.

(B) Sell it at a garage sale.

(C) Give it to family, friends, Goodwill or the Salvation Army.

(D) If nothing else works, take it to the dump and throw it away

It won't be easy, in fact it may be as painful as hell, but in the tiny space of a car or van, everything has to be useful, so keep getting rid of stuff until it will all fit in the vehicle you choose to live in.

I got rid of everything I could, and it was still twice as much as could fit in my box van. So I did it again and made even harder choices. That cut it down by about half, but still too much to fit in the van. So I did it again and again until it would all finally fit. Today I am so glad I did it. I am free, I own things and they don't own me.

Keep working on paring down your stuff and let's move onto the next step into your new life of vandwelling.

SETTING PRIORITIES:

Your next step is to decide which kind of vehicle you are going to live in. Because we are all so different there is no one best vehicle for you to live in. I live in a very simple 6 foot by 10 foot trailer and it makes me very happy, but it might make you miserable. Before you do anything else you have to take stock of your individual priorities and needs and decide where you are and where you are going.

The reason this is so important is that no vehicle does everything well so you are going to have to make compromises. For example, I would love the comfort of a motor home, but I can't afford to pay for the huge amount of gas they burn and a top priority to me is being able to get into the backcountry of National Forests and BLM desert land. By knowing what is most important to me, I can buy the vehicle that makes me happiest. The answers to these questions will help you set priorities for your future life of vandwelling:

1-How much time do you have to get ready?

A person who just got a 30 day eviction notice and has to move into his/her vehicle right now has one top priority, get a roof over your head quickly. Their choice will be very different than a person who wants to move into a van but has to sell his house first. The first person has to buy the best thing he can as soon as he can, the second can look for as long as it takes to get the best possible deal on the perfect vehicle

2-How much money do you have, and where will it be coming from?

For example, a person who has no money doesn't have to look for and buy a vehicle because he can't afford a new one. He is going to move into the one he has now. But another person may need to plan for her plumbing business so her priority is to find a box van, box truck or cargo trailer that is large enough she can both live in and work out of. Another fellow may be retiring with a good pension, so he will be looking for a nice RV to live in for the rest of his life. How much you can spend will determine which vehicle you buy.

3-Will you be living in a city, boondocking in the country, or traveling?

If you are going to live in a city, then being able to park without being hassled will be your top priority, so stealth will be your main concern. If you are going to be boondocking in the country then stealth isn't important to you at all but maybe you will want four-wheel drive to get further into the back-country. Or, if you are going to be traveling a lot, then gas mileage will be a top priority for you.

4-Will your vehicle be your home, or just a bedroom?

Some people sleep in their vans, but they spend their days somewhere else. They spend their days at work, the park, restaurants, libraries, Barnes and Nobles, the mall, friends, family, anywhere but in their van. Others, like me, spend just as much time in their van as they did when they lived in a house. If your van is just a bedroom, you won't need as much room and comfort as the person who spends most of their day in the van.

5-How much comfort do you need?

This is a really hard question for most of us to answer, but answering it honestly will determine whether you love or hate living in a vehicle. If you absolutely have to take a shower every day or you are miserable, and you fail to plan for one, then you will hate living in a car or van without a shower.

The best way to answer the question is to go camping. In many ways, living in a car or van is very much like going camping. The only real difference is instead of setting up a tent, you sleep in the van. If you have done much camping, did you enjoy it? Were you okay without a shower every day? Did you mind being without all the comforts of home? Did you feel naked without four walls? If you haven't done much camping, go camping! Go as often as you can. Try to make it as similar to living in a van as you practically can.

Another option to help determine your need for comfort is to practice in your apartment. The first step is to move into your bedroom and stop using the rest of the house; don't use the kitchen, living room or bathroom, instead, perform all their functions in your bedroom. Right now that seems impossible, but later in the book I will show you how to do all those things in your bedroom or van, so read the whole book before you try this experiment.

You can make the experiment even more realistic by making a mock-up of a van in your apartment. First, go to a used car lot and find a van the size you are planning on buying. Use a tape measure to get the inside dimensions of the living area, excluding the drivers area. Let's say it measures 6 foot by 10 foot. Next, get some big cardboard boxes and use them to make a 6 foot by 10 foot space in the corner of your bedroom. Now move into your cardboard "van." Instead of living in the bedroom you will live in your little cardboard van. The more realistic you make it, the better you will understand what comfort level you need in your vehicle home.

By answering these questions, you should know more about what your future life as a vandweller will be like, and what you are looking for in a vehicle home. Next we will take that knowledge and decide which vehicle to buy.

WHAT KIND OF VEHICLE TO BUY?

After honestly looking at your needs and priorities, you should know enough to choose a vehicle. First, you must understand that there is no perfect vehicle. Every vehicle will be a compromise between its pluses and minuses. It will give you what you want in one area, but not much of something else in another. For example, we all want lots of room and comfort and great gas mileage, but that doesn't exist. A minivan will give you gas mileage in the mid-twenties, but has very little room. A full-size RV has all the room and comfort we could want but will probably get much less than 10 mpg. Now you can see why setting priorities is so important, you can only get some of what you want in your vehicle home, and some things you can't get at all, so you must know what your priorities are. Let's look at the different criteria we need to consider:

1-Stealth Ability:

Generally, society frowns on people who don't conform. Sometimes it does more than frown; it can hassle you, fine you, and even throw you in jail for living in a vehicle in a city. The best way to avoid these problems is to not be noticed. If the authorities don't know you are living in a van, they won't hassle you. We call that stealth parking. If you are going to live and work in a city, then this is very important and you need to make it your highest priority.

2-Room and Comfort:

Hopefully you have been really honest with yourself and you know how much room and comfort you need. The key issues are (A) Shower (B) Flush toilet (C) Air conditioning (D) Heating. If you need these, then a Class B or a larger RV is your best choice. But, if stealth is your highest priority and comfort is a very close second, then a box/step van would be a better choice. It will give you great stealth and enough room to add all the comforts you need. On the other hand, if you can compromise on room and comfort, then you may be okay in a van.

3-Headroom:

I know lots of people who live in vans who don't mind their low height at all. They claim they get used to crawling around, hunched over to do everything in their vans. But I can't do it. Being able to stand up in any vehicle I live in is a top priority. That's why I bought a box van instead of a regular van; I wanted the extra space and headroom. If you need more headroom and stealth, a conversion van with a high-top is your best choice.

4-Initial Cost:

The one vehicle that offers the best compromise on all these things is a Dodge/Mercedes Sprinter. It gets 22 mpg from its little diesel engine, has lots of space and headroom and yet remains quite stealthy. But, even used it will cost at least $20,000. On the other hand, an older Dodge van with a 318 V8 can be bought for $2,000 and will get from 15-19 mpg, has a good amount of room and is very stealthy. If you only have $2,000, then your choice is easy, you buy the older Dodge van.

5-Fuel Economy:

Of course you want the best fuel economy you can get, but you have to be ready to make compromises. Look at the example above of the two Dodge vans. The Dodge Sprinter will cost you $18,000 more than the gas engine Dodge van. It will get 4-5 more miles per gallon than the gas engine, but diesel costs more per gallon, and the diesel engine will cost much more when it needs repairs. How many miles will you have to drive before you get that initial $18,000 extra cost back? My guess is that it is in the millions of miles. You will probably never recoup that extra money you spent. Keep that idea in mind when you factor in fuel economy.

Something else to consider is comfort versus fuel economy. For example, a minivan may get 20-25 mpg, and a full size van may get 15-19 mpg. But, the full-size van has a great deal more room and may have a high-top. Only you can decide if the loss of comfort is worth the savings in fuel economy.

6-Back-Road Ability:

This will only be important if you are like me and spend most of your time on public land and want to go further into the back-country. I frequently follow little dirt roads that take me far back into the mountains or desert, so I have a four-wheel drive pickup and nothing else will do. You might think that a minivan with all-wheel drive will do just as well. But ground clearance is as important as four-wheel drive, and minivans have very little ground clearance. There are lots of places where they will get high-centered long before they run out of traction.

NOW LET'S EVALUATE DIFFERENT VEHICLES BASED ON THESE CRITERIA:

MOTORCYCLE: When I retired and started full-timing, I strongly considered living out of a Honda Gold wing motorcycle. I would pull a trailer which would let me carry enough stuff to camp on public land. However, I love dogs and there was no practical way to have a dog on a motorcycle, so I gave up on the idea. But that doesn't mean it is a bad idea, it just wasn't for me. If you love adventure and fun, a motorcycle could be for you.

- **Stealth:** Nonexistent. Since you have to set up a tent or have a pop-up trailer, everybody knows you are living in your motorcycle.

- **Room and Comfort:** Nonexistent. You are tent camping with the minimum of extras.

- **Headroom:** All you could want! There is nothing over your head but the elements.

- **Initial Cost:** Fairly low. Older bikes can be reasonable, newer ones are surprisingly expensive.

- **Fuel Economy:** Outstanding! Any bike should be able to get 30-40 mpg and some will give you 50-60 or more, depending on how heavy they are.

- **Back-road ability:** The big heavy touring bikes aren't so good, but BMW makes some touring bikes that are very good on the back-roads. The 650cc dual-sport bikes are outstanding off-road.

- **Who it's for:** Anyone looking for adventure and fun along with great gas mileage.

CAR: If you don't have much money or time, a car can work. But a minivan or SUV has much more room and comfort and can get nearly as good fuel economy.

- **Stealth**: A car has excellent stealth. No one expects someone to be living in a car. Their one problem is privacy; it's hard to stretch your body out to sleep without being seen.

- **Room and Comfort:** While some cars have more room than others, none of them have much room. You would either have to be an extreme minimalist or keep a storage place to live in a car. Comfort is non-existent.

- **Headroom:** Very little!

- **Initial Cost**: You probably already have a car, so the initial cost will be free, you can't do better than that!! If you have to buy one, it will be cheaper than anything else.

- **Fuel Economy:** Smaller cars can get wonderful gas mileage.

- **Back-road ability:** Very poor. Even four/all wheel drive cars will be limited by their low clearance.

- **Who it's for:** (A) The person who has very limited money or time. You can move into your car and start saving towards buying something larger. (B) I have a friend who takes multi-month trips around the country in her Toyota Prius. She loves it! It holds all she needs, is easy to drive, and gets 45 mpg.

It allows her to travel when she couldn't afford to otherwise. (C) A person who lives by tent-camping on public land like National Forests or BLM desert land, can be happy with a car. Essentially, you are backpacking, except your car is the backpack, and a car is huge compared to a backpack. I think it is a very good choice for a minimalist who travels the country living on public land.

SUV: I have a friend who lives in a Ford Explorer in Denver, and he loves it. It has great stealth, and the high-clearance four-wheel drive is great in snowstorms.

- **Stealth:** Very good, no one thinks someone would be living in a SUV.

- **Room:** The big models like the Suburban and Excursion have quite a bit of room; the smallest models have very little room.

- **Headroom:** Low. None of them are available with high-tops, so there is very little headroom.

- **Initial Cost:** Fair. SUV's hold their value better than cars or vans so you will need more money to buy one.

- **Fuel Economy**: The small and medium models can get pretty good mileage, but the V8 engines will be poor to fair. The largest models are available with diesel engines and they can get decent mileage.

- **Back-road ability:** Outstanding! Some aren't intended for off-road use, but those that are, are very, very good at it. They can be modified to be even better. An SUV will open up a lot more of the National Forest and desert for you to explore and live on.

- **Who it's for:** Mainly those who want the high-clearance four-wheel drive in snow country and off-road use. A four-wheel drive Suburban or Excursion with a diesel engine will go deep into the back-country, get decent mileage, and have quite a bit of room. They are also able to pull a very large, heavy trailer.

MINI-VAN: I know many people who live in mini-vans and love them. They are a very good compromise of stealth, room and fuel economy.

- **Stealth:** Outstanding! Nobody expects a soccer-mom to be living in a minivan,

so they just blend into the background
and don't attract attention.

- **Room and comfort:** Adequate. They are
  small, but a person who has minimal
  needs can live in one with no problem.

- **Headroom:** Adequate. There aren't many
  high-top conversion minivans, so you are
  going to have to live with the low roofs.

- **Initial Cost:** There are lots of used
  minivans out there so you should
  be able to find a good deal.

- **Fuel Economy:** Very good! Most minivans
  should be able to get from 18-25 mpg.

- **Back-road ability:** Average. They are often
  available with All-Wheel drive, but the
  low clearance can be a big problem.

- **Who it's for:** Anyone who needs to
  give up the extra room of a full-size
  van for the better gas mileage.

FULL-SIZE VAN: By far the best all-around
choice!! Surprisingly good gas mileage, lots of room
and very good stealth make them a winner.

- **Stealth:** Very good, but not quite as good as a car, SUV or minivan. There are so many vans around that nobody really notices them, but many law enforcement officers are aware that there are people who live in their vans.

- **Room and comfort:** Very good, you should be able to live comfortably in one. The extended length vans are relatively huge inside.

- **Headroom:** Good. You should be able to find a high-top conversion van that will make living in a van much more comfortable.

- **Initial Cost:** Good. There are enough used vans for sale that you should be able to find one that fits your budget.

- **Fuel Economy:** Surprisingly good. Most late model vans can get 15-19 mpg or better.

- **Back-road ability:** Fairly good. Vans with four-wheel drive are rare and expensive. Ground clearance on 2wd vans is slightly above average.

- **Who it's for:** Everyone, they are the best all-around choice. However, if you need the best fuel economy you can get, then a minivan is better, or if you need more room and comfort a Class B or an RV will be better.

CLASS - B: This is a van that has been converted to have all (or most of) the comforts of an RV. Generally, they will have a shower, toilet, and kitchenette. Sometimes they will even have a generator, air conditioning, and a furnace. They have much more comfort than a van, but less stealth, and slightly worse fuel economy.

- **Stealth:** Fair. Generally they look like an RV, so people will think someone may be living in there.

- **Room and comfort:** Very good. The only thing more comfortable is a full-size RV.

- **Headroom:** Very good. Generally you should be able to stand upright in one.

- **Initial Cost:** Fair. Class B's hold their value very well. Finding one that is affordable can be difficult.

- **Fuel Economy:** Good. The extra weight, and generally a bigger engine means their fuel economy won't be as good as a regular van, but much better than any other RV.

- **Back-road ability:** Poor. They are intended for paved roads.

- **Who it's for:** Anyone who needs more comfort than a van can provide but better fuel economy than a RV.

BOX/STEP VAN: I lived in a box van for six years and loved it. They are a great choice because they are very large and you can make them into anything you want.

- **Stealth:** Very Good. Box and step vans look normal in any commercial/ industrial location like malls or big box stores. However, they look out of place in a residential area.

- **Room and Comfort:** Very good. Most are 8 foot wide by 12-14 foot long, and can be as long as 16 feet. With all that room you can be as comfortable as you want.

- **Headroom:** Outstanding. Most are 7-8 feet tall.

- **Fuel Economy:** Poor to Fair. Gas engines will get 5-8 mpg while diesel engines will get 10-12 mpg. An exception is Cummins 4 or 6 cylinder diesel engines commonly available in step vans. They get 17-20 mpg and are legendary for their long-life.

- **Initial Cost:** I paid $1,500 for mine, and a friend paid $4,500 for a 2001 Ford with a 7.3 liter diesel, so chances are you can find one you can afford.

- **Back-Road Ability:** Poor

- **Who It's For:** Anyone who wants room and comfort and great stealth. They are especially good for couples and families. The extra room can be handy for people who work out of their vans and people who want to haul motorcycles, boats or ATV's.

PICKUP WITH SHELL OR CAMPER: The biggest problem with pickups is you have to get out and walk around to get in the shell/camper. That ruins your stealth and can be unsafe. If there is something outside that is scaring you, in a van you just get in the front seat and drive away. With a pickup you have to get out and walk around to the cab, possibly increasing the danger.

- **Stealth:** Fair. Walking around and getting in the shell/camper ruins your stealth.

- **Room and comfort:** Poor to great. If you are living in a shell, you can't have much comfort. If you have a big slide-in camper, they are very comfortable with all the comforts of home.

- **Headroom:** Poor to great. See above.

- **Initial Cost:** There are lots of used pickups around so you should be able to get a good deal.

- **Fuel Economy:** Poor to Great. Many older pickups get 8-12 mpg. A Ford 300 in-line six can get 19-20 mpg and a Dodge Cummins diesel can get 20-22 mpg.

- **Back-road ability:** Very good. Pickups with high clearance and four-wheel drive are commonly available and will get you far into the back-country.

- **Who it's for:** They are the best choice for anyone who wants to get far back into the back-country with more comfort than an SUV.

RECREATIONAL VEHICLES (RV):

- **Stealth:** Non-existent. Everyone will know there is a person sleeping in there.

- **Room and Comfort:** Outstanding. An RV will give you all the comforts of home

- **Headroom:** Outstanding. Plenty of headroom for even the tallest person.

- **Initial Cost:** High. While you can get a 1970's Class C for as low as $1,500 a newer model will be much more.

- **Fuel Economy:** Miserable. 5-10 mpg is standard.

- **Back-road ability:** Non existent. Don't even think about it.

- **Who it's for:** Anyone who wants comfort above all else.

Different Types of RV's: The main consideration with RV's is their terrible fuel economy. There are two main solutions: (A) Pull an economy car behind the RV or (B) Tow your trailer with a diesel pickup that gets decent fuel economy. A towed car gets better fuel economy, but now you have two vehicles to maintain and pay insurance on. A diesel pickup is noisy and smelly and generally doesn't get great fuel economy.

- **Class C:** This is a RV with a van nose and an overhead cab with a bed. Its main advantage is a familiar driving position. You will need to tow a car to save money on gas and not have to break camp for day trips.

- **Class A:** This RV looks something like a bus with a flat front nose. It has a very unfamiliar driving position. You will need to tow a car to save money on gas and not have to break camp for day trips.

- **Pop-Up Trailer:** These are very light and so they can be towed by a car or SUV, giving you better fuel economy. They are pretty comfortable and can be bought for a reasonable price. However, most have fabric sides which will eventually rot or mildew, are susceptible to animal damage and are cold in the winter. There is a brand called A-Liner that makes a hard-sided pop-up that looks great but they cost more. Once you have set up camp, you can drive the tow vehicle on day trips without breaking camp.

- **Travel Trailer:** These trailers hook up to the trailer hitch of a pickup (or SUV with the smaller, lighter models), leaving the bed of the truck available to carry more stuff. Older ones can be bought very cheaply and have all the comforts of home. They are not as easy to drive as a fifth wheels and not as stable at speed. Once you have set up camp, you can drive the tow vehicle on day trips without breaking camp.

- **Fifth Wheel Trailer:** These trailers track much better than Travel Trailers and are easier to drive and back up. However, the hitch in the bed of the pickup takes up much of its storage space. Once you have set up camp, you can drive the tow vehicle on day trips without breaking camp.

MY RECOMMENDATIONS:

1-Best all-around choice: full-size van.

They have great stealth, good gas mileage, and have plenty of room. Buy a conversion van or a high-top van and you get enough headroom. I have a friend with a high-top extended cargo van and it looks like a mansion in there; all the room you could need. Cargo vans have slightly better stealth, but a conversion van with a high-top is more comfortable. Unless you have very specific needs, buy a full-size van. My personal choice would be a 1996 or newer Dodge conversion van with a high-top and a 318 V8.

2-If you need the best fuel economy with decent comfort: mini-van.

A mini-van will give you better gas mileage than a full-size van, but with much less room. To me, it isn't a good trade, but for many people it is, especially those that travel a lot. My personal choice would be a 1996 or newer Chevrolet Astro minivan.

3-If you need more comfort with decent gas mileage: Class B.

A Class B adds a huge amount of comfort and only slightly cuts your gas mileage. If you don't mind the loss of stealth, they are an outstanding choice. They cost more than the equivalent van, but if you tried to add all the comforts they have to a plain van, the total cost would be much, much more.

4-If you want room and comfort with great stealth: Box/Step Van.

If you can live with the poor gas mileage, box/ step vans give you lots of room with great stealth. They are especially appropriate for couples, families and the self-employed. In my opinion, your very best choice is a Ford with a 7.3 liter diesel engine, or a step van with a Cummins 4 or 6 cylinder diesel. One caution, not all box vans have a pass-through from the drivers area to the box in back. Make sure the one you buy has one.

5-If you want room and comfort at any cost: RV.

An RV gives you all the comfort of home but at a high cost: they have terrible gas mileage and stealth. If you can live with that, they are a super choice. I have a friend who lives in a 1978 Class C and loves it. He tows a Ford Festiva, a small car that gets 40 mpg. He works as a campground host in the winter and lives in the desert in the winter. Since he only drives the RV a few thousand miles a year (he drives the Festiva mostly) and camps on public land instead of stealth parking in the city, the bad gas mileage and poor stealth don't matter to him at all. He gets all the comfort of home with virtually no negatives. His example is something to strongly consider.

6-If you want the best back-road ability with comfort: Four Wheel Drive Pickup

If you boondock in the mountains or the desert, a four wheel drive pickup is your best choice. A tall camper shell or a slide in camper can be very comfortable. With a slide-in camper or a trailer, you can take the camper off or drop the trailer, and set up camp and go four-wheeling with the empty pickup. My personal choice is a Dodge Cummins Diesel Pickup which will give you 15-22 mpg, depending on if it is empty, has a slide-in camper, or is pulling a trailer. A close second is a Ford with a 7.3 liter diesel. It's a good reliable engine, but its fuel economy isn't nearly as good as the Dodge with a Cummins.

HOW TO BUY A VEHICLE:

Now that you know which vehicle you want to live in, the next question is which model should you buy? One question I hear all the time is, "Which model is the best, and which one should I avoid?" That is a valid question, because some models and engines develop a good or bad reputation and we should look for the first and avoid the latter. For example, the Ford 7.3 liter diesel has a great reputation and I would gladly buy one. On the other hand, when Ford replaced the 7.3 with the 6.0 liter diesel, it has a bad reputation of having constant problems. I would never buy one. But this kind of black and white reputations is very unusual. Most of today's engines are quite good. With very few exceptions, any well-maintained engine will serve you well. Here are my three critical rules for buying a vehicle which are much more important than considering its reputation:

1) Get it checked out by a mechanic first.

2) Never buy a vehicle without getting it checked out by a mechanic first.

3) Paying a mechanic to check out a vehicle before you buy it is the best money you will ever spend.

Are you getting the idea? Don't buy a used vehicle without getting it checked out by a mechanic first. Let me tell you a true story. I once bought a Ford F150 pickup. It had a 300 in-line 6 cylinder engine with a 4 speed overdrive stick-shift transmission. The 300 has one of the best reputations of any engine ever made. It is a great engine that everyone told me would run forever. So I bought the truck based on its reputation and didn't get it checked out by a mechanic.

I loved the gas mileage, it got 20 mpg on the freeway, but it was constant problems. Its previous owners hadn't taken care of it and the engine was worn out with 150,000 miles on it. The clutch, brakes and front-end went out on it. The cost of repairs was going to be many thousands of dollars, much more than the truck was worth. I gave it away for free to a friend who was going to find the parts in junk yards and do all the work himself.

Had I taken it to a mechanic before I bought it, I could have saved myself thousands of dollars. A mechanic would have listened to the engine, looked at the brakes and front-end, and felt the clutch and told me it was a piece of junk, a hole to pour money in. Never buy a vehicle based on reputation alone. Much more important is how well the vehicle was maintained by its previous owners, and only a mechanic can tell you that.

My next advice is to buy as new a vehicle as you can afford. Many people lament the "good old days" when engines were simple and there were no "computers." In my opinion, they are dead wrong! Today's engines are far superior to the engines of decades ago. They make more power, get far better gas mileage and are much more reliable. An engine from the 1970s would need to be rebuilt after 100,000 miles, got 10 mpg and polluted like crazy. Today you should easily get 200,000 miles or more, get 15-50 mpg and burn very cleanly.

One of the most important reasons for these advances is fuel injection. If at all possible, you don't want a, carburetor, you want fuel injection. A second major advance occurred in 1996 when nearly all vehicles were required to have OBD II. That stands for On Board Diagnostics, second edition. Essentially it is the computer that controls the engine and lets it make more power, pollute less, and get better gas mileage. Just as important, it lets any mechanic plug into the computer and know the exact status of the engine.

Bottom Line: buy a 1996 or newer vehicle if at all possible with the fewest number of miles your budget will allow and get it checked out by a mechanic before you buy.

HOW TO FIND YOUR NEW VEHICLE:

I know many people who had a hard time finding a good deal on a good van. I wish there was a magic secret to find one, but it is just perseverance and patience. Keep looking, it's out there waiting for you. There are four main ways to search for your new vehicle-home:

1-Craigslist.com:

You are more likely to find your new home on wheels on craigslist than any other way. It's free, easy and it works great, what more could you want? If you've never used craigslist, just do a Google search with the key words "craigslist" and the name of the nearest large town.

For example, if you lived in a small town 30 miles from Nashville, you would type "Nashville craigslist" into the search bar of your web browser. The Nashville craigslist will come up as the first choice. Just click on it and you will get to the home page. From there select autos for sale. Craigslist lets you set search terms. For example, you could type in: "dodge cummins diesel," and all the ads that had those words would come up. Or you could type: "ford 7.3 diesel van." I love craigslist!

One problem with craigslist, is that you can only search one city at a time. To solve that problem, several websites have popped up to offer nationwide searches. My favorite is http: //www. searchtempest.com/. It allows you to enter a zip code and set how far away from it craigslist should search. For example, if your zip code is 93664, you can enter that and tell it to search everything within 250 miles. You can enter any distance in miles you are willing to drive to look at a vehicle. Here are other websites that offer nationwide craigslist searches:

- http: //www.searchtempest.com/

- http: //www.craigs-list-search.com/

- http: //crazedlist.org/

- http: //www.allofcraigslist.org/

- http: //craigspal.com

2-Local newspaper or Penney-saver:

The internet has really cut into local newspapers classified advertising. Why pay for it when it's free on craigslist? However, I think they are still worth checking out. If you never find anything, then you may want to stop looking in them and stick to craigslist exclusively.

3-Used Car Dealer:

Lots of people will tell you not to even consider used car dealers, but I think you should check them out as long as you are sure you can withstand a salesman's high-pressure pitch. I bought my current pickup from a used car dealer seven years ago, and I was delighted by the deal. I had it checked out by a mechanic who said it was in great shape and the dealer let me put $3,000 down and financed $2,000. It allowed me to buy a better vehicle than I could have otherwise. That said, I'm sure I will buy my next vehicle off of craigslist.

4-Ebay:

I've never bought a vehicle off ebay.com, but I know several people who have and they said it worked really well. The one rule I have is to never buy a vehicle without having it checked out by a mechanic first. That may be hard to do with ebay.

GETTING READY TO MOVE IN;

So you are in the process of getting rid of all your stuff and you've found just the right van at just the right price: now what? It may seem simple, but turning that tiny space into a home can be overwhelming. As you approach converting the van into your home there are two possible methods:

1) **Left Brain:** Plan everything, right down to the tiniest detail, and then build the van. Once it is all done, move in.

2) **Right Brain:** Throw a sleeping pad and sleeping bag down on the floor, pile a

> duffle bag full of clothes and your other possessions in the corner, and move in

I may be exaggerating, but some people really do carry it that far. Which way is better? I've done it both ways. My first night in a van I literally just put a sleeping pad and bag on the floor and that was it; I was home. From that humble beginning, I started planning and building until the van become a very cozy, pleasant little home.

In the little trailer I live in now, I did just the opposite. I planned the lay-out in great detail, and then built it. When I was done, I moved in. Neither way is right or wrong; in fact I think it has more to do with your personality than anything else. Left brained, engineering types are more comfortable with detailed plans and right-brained, creative people are sometimes more comfortable with a looser, evolutionary process.

If this is your first time living in a van, I think you are better to err on the side of too little planning instead of too much planning. Sitting and looking at an empty van is very different than living in one. The ideas that seem great on paper may be terrible in actual living. My general advice is to move into your van with the minimum of preparation. Then, after you've lived in it for a while, you will start to see the problems you are facing, and find solutions. That will give you enough knowledge to do your detailed build. But again, this is just general advice, you need to do whatever makes you most comfortable.

Please understand, I'm not suggesting you not make any plans or preparations. This is one time when the old saying, "Those who fail to plan, can plan to fail" is very true. I know many people who just throw a huge pile of stuff in their van and move in. They have to move all the stuff around constantly to find something they need. There is barely enough room to sleep, so they have to throw a bunch of it up in the front seats just to be able to lay their bed out. Then the next morning they have to move it all back to drive. It's a very miserable way to live, so they get discouraged and quit. I don't want that to happen to you.

On the other hand, I've seen people get so frustrated about how to get the van ready they became virtually paralyzed with fear of doing it wrong. We need to find a middle way. So in the rest of this chapter, I'm going to give you simple, step-by-step directions about how-to get your van ready to live in. These steps are based on priority, first-things-first. You don't have to do them all You'll have to decide for yourself when you have done enough, and now is the time to move in and hit the road.

1-Pull out the seats: The first step is pretty obvious, if your van has seats in the back, they have to come out. Some conversion vans come with a back seat that folds down into a bed. You may be tempted to keep it, but I suggest that you remove it as well. There are two reasons I say that: 1) Their design makes it hard to use the space under them for storage. When you have that little space, you can't afford to waste any of it. 2) They are uncomfortable. This is going to be your new home and the one thing you are going to want is a bed that gives you a good night's sleep, so rip that coach-bed out, and get one that will be easy to sleep on.

There are so many variables about how seats are mounted that I can't really give you much advice on how to remove the seats. If it seems too difficult, or you don't have the right tools, take it to an auto repair or auto body shop and pay someone to take them out for you

2-Cover the windows: The next most important thing you must do is cover the windows so you have privacy. You don't want people walking by and seeing you changing clothes or sleeping in the van. That's a sure path to trouble. Another consideration is that in the summer, heat will pour in through the window and in the winter warmth will escape through the glass.

There is a miracle product that is going to take care of both problems called *Reflectix*. I highly recommend you cover all your windows with it. It is a piece of bubble wrap sandwiched between two layers of heavy aluminum foil material. You can't see through it and it works extremely well to keep the heat out in summer and in during the winter. There are four common ways to install it:

1-Duct Tape:

Taping it to the walls works well, but it is ugly and hard to take on and off, it can also leave a gummy mess, especially in the summer sun. If you have windows that you want to cover permanently, it is a good choice. Just be sure to cut the Reflectix larger than the glass so the duct tape is as far as possible from the heat generated in the window. That helps minimize the tape getting gummy.

2-Two-sided Velcro Tape:

There are times when you will want to take the Reflectix off the windows (when you drive, for example). Velcro works great for that because it makes it easy to take the Reflectix on and off. Buy the highest quality you can so it won't peel off with use. Applying it is as simple as peeling the backing off the tape and apply it to the Reflectix and around the window frame. Again, cut the Reflectix as large as possible and put the Velcro tape as far as possible from the glass so it won't get hot and peel off.

3-Magnets:

Magnets also allow you to hold the Reflectix in place and then easily take it on and off. You will need very strong rare earth magnets which you can buy at craft stores or Amazon.com. Duct tape the magnets to the corners of the Reflectix. If you have a cargo van with bare metal walls, then the magnets will stick to the walls. If you don't have metal walls you can duct tape large metal washers to the wall, lining them up with the magnets.

4-Compression:

It's possible to cut the Reflectix slightly larger than the window and just press it into the frame around the glass and have it stay. This works surprisingly well. But if you take it in and out a lot, it will eventually lose its shape and start falling out.

3-Make a divider between the front driving area and the back living area: This is important for the same reasons you need to cover the windows: people walking by can see inside and all the glass up front lets in huge amounts of heat in during the summer and out in the winter. One simple way to hang a curtain is with an expanding shower curtain rod. They twist out to expand and lock in place. Another option is to use a curtain rod. You want to use a heavy fabric that will block both light and heat from getting through.

I also recommend a second layer of either Reflectix or a space blanket to act as insulation and a vapor barrier. The curve of the roof makes it hard to get a tight seal along the top, but the tighter the seal the better. One way to match the curve is with a long piece of cardboard and trim it down till it follows close to the roof. Use that as a pattern to trim the Reflectix or the curtains to fit flush to the roof.

4-Flooring: With the back seats out, now is the time to plan for a floor covering. Some people get really elaborate with the floor, but I've never understood that. In my opinion the floor is always going to be cold no matter what you do, so I think the less you do the better. I suggest you just find a cheap carpet, throw it down and call it good.

If you want something a little more elaborate, you can cut plywood to fit around the wheel-wells and put the carpet over the plywood. Some people buy a sheet of linoleum, cut it to fit and glue it to the plywood. Linoleum looks nice, is very tough and is easy to clean. Another option is to put wood flooring such as hardwood or bamboo on the plywood.

5-Insulation: No matter where you live, at some point you are going to be in extremes of weather (heat or cold) so I think adding insulation is important. There are so many variables in different make, models and years of van, I can't get too detailed about the how-to of insulation but I can give you some direction on which insulation to use. You have three primary choices:

1–Styrofoam:

Let me just tell you that I believe styrofoam is by far your best choice. It is cheap, light, easy to work with and has a fairly high R value. It can be installed with glue or you can screw 1x3 boards across the walls and screw the plywood into it. The pink or blue styrofoam is better than the white. The thinner pieces like ½ or ¾ inch thick sheets will bend to conform to the curve of the walls and roof. If you want more insulation, just add multiple layers.

2-Blown-In Foam:

I've never used the blow-in foam, but I know it is expensive and hard to install. It does have a higher R value than the other choices. To me it violates the KISS principle, but I know people who have done it and think it is the best way to go

3-Fiberglass:

Fiberglass is cheap but unpleasant to work with. To install it you will need to build stud-type walls to hold the batts. Standard batts are 3 ½ inches thick to go between 2x4 stud walls. If you put it on the walls, you will loose 7 inches of interior space which is just too much. You will be tempted to squeeze it in taking less space, but you shouldn't compress it or you will greatly decrease it's R value. I think it is a poor choice.

After you are done insulating, the easiest way to finish the walls is with paneling. It is light, cheap and easy to work with. Some people cover it by gluing carpeting or fabric on top of it, but that is a matter of personal taste.

6-**Start studying other van conversions.** With the seats out, now is the time, to start researching the web for different layouts of van conversions. There are many different examples on my two sites, http: // cheaprvliving.comm and http: //cheapgreenrvliving.com/ index.html. Another great source of photos is the Yahoo group "Vandwellers." Join the group here: http: //autos.groups.yahoo.com/group/VanDwellers/. After you join the group, search the photo album where you will find a huge variety of van conversions with lots of ingenious, creative ideas. Take your laptop out to the van and hang out in it while looking at the pictures of different floor-plans. Think about how you would like to lay out the van.

7-**Decide where the bed will go:** One of the most important decisions you have to make is where you will put the bed so look specifically for how other people placed their beds. Basically, you have two choices: (A)along the wall, or (B)across the back in front of the back door. Personally, I think across the back is best because you can reach the storage space under the bed from the rear doors or from the front. If you are tall, you can make the bed wider and sleep at a diagonal across the bed so you can stretch all the way out. The wider bed also leaves room so that if you ever 'entertain: company, they will fit in the bed with you. My last bed was 48 inches wide (the width of a piece of plywood) and it worked really well for me. It left a huge amount of room underneath for storage that was easily accessed from front or back. But that is just my opinion, I know many people who choose to put it along the wall behind the driver's seat. If you are very tall, you really don't have a choice it must go along the wall.

You don't have to decide right now, so just spend time in the van using your imagination and go through your daily activities in your mind. With the bed across the back, where will everything go? Where would it go with the bed along the side? How will you get dressed, cook meals or go to the bathroom. Eventually you are going to have to decide on a layout but for now you are just using your imagination.

8-Organizing Your Stuff: You've heard the old saying, "A place for everything, and everything in its place?" Well that is doubly true when you live in a space as tiny as a van. You must find a way to organize your possessions, or your mobile life will be a nightmare. The best way to organize is with built-in cabinets and storage areas. Why is that true? Because you can regain all the wasted vertical space along the top of the walls. But if you don't have the time, money or knowledge to do it right now, you can still move in and add it later as you are able. There are three good ways to organize right now:

1-Duffle Bags:

You should be able to find some duffle type bags pretty cheap at Target or Wal-Mart. They work great for clothes (as long as you don't mind if they get wrinkled) because there is no wasted space. Plus, as you take clothes out, the bag gets smaller and doesn't waste space. But that's not all they are good for. I carry winter and summer clothes so whichever one is out of season stays in a duffel bag. I also carry extra towels, sheets and blankets and they are in duffels when not needed. All these things do well in duffels because the fabric breaths and things don't get moldy or stale in the bags.

If you build a wide bed across the back of the van and sleep diagonally, you can throw the duffle bags in the unused corners and regain that space. You can also put hooks near the roof of the van and hang the duffels from the ceiling, regaining some wasted space.

Some people prefer compression sacks to duffel bags. They are sacks with built in straps that let you compress the contents down to a much smaller space. They work very well but leave the items in them very wrinkled and the compression can damage most insulation materials. Wal-Mart and all sporting goods store sell them.

2-Plastic Organizers:

Nothing works as well for organizing a van as plastic totes and drawers. They are cheap, light and very tough. In every vehicle I have ever lived in I have had a large assortment of plastic organizers. In my current converted cargo trailer I have eight Rubbermaid 18 gallon Totes. I find them so useful I designed the whole structure around them. Four of them are under my bed and hold things I don't need to get to very often, once a month or less. The other four our out where I can get to them quicker and I put things in them that I use daily or weekly. I also have nine different drawer units in four different sizes. The smallest has three drawers that are 2 inch by 7 inches, the next size has three drawers which are 3 inch by 10 inch, then I have four, single drawer units that are 9 by 15 inches. Finally there is a three drawer unit that has 8 by 20 inch drawers. I designed the trailer specifically to fit those drawer units. Between the various sizes all my stuff is very organized and I don't have to waste a lot of time searching for things. When I want something, I just walk over, open the drawer, and there it is. I strongly encourage you to use plastic totes and drawers for organizing your van. Target has the broadest selection of plastic organizers.

3-Used dressers and desks from thrift stores:

I know several people that did this. They found dressers and desks at a thrift store that fit perfectly in their van and which gives them instant organization. It also gives the van a homey feeling they were looking for. A roll-top type desk with plenty of drawers and an upper shelf is especially good at using space efficiently. Some computer desks have upper shelves and lots of drawers so they are a great find. Just be sure to measure to see how tall the desk can be and still fit under the roof, or you may have to return it.

It's easy to secure them to the floor so they don't go flying in an accident. Just go to Home Depot and buy "L" brackets (2-4 inches, depending on the furniture) and sheet metal screws. I prefer the self-tapping kind with hex heads. Put a nut driver in your drill and they screw into the floor or wall very easily. Screw one side of the "L" into the bottom of the furniture, and the other side of the "L" into the floor. Be sure the screw is short enough that it can't go through the floor and into something important, like the gas tank! To be double safe you can use an "L" bracket to go from the top of the furniture to the wall. Because of the curve of the walls, you will need a long "L" to reach the wall. You will have to measure to see how long it needs to be.

9-What if I'm not a carpenter or handyman: In today's world many of us are growing up without learning many practical skills. Most of us can't work on our cars or build things with tools. I've had people tell me that they would like to live in a vehicle, but because they lack practical skills they don't think they can. They're afraid of what might happen if they break down.

I look at it this way, when I used to live in a house, if there was an electrical problem, I called an electrician, if there was a plumbing problem, I called a plumber. If the roof leaked, I called a roofer. Well, in the same way if I live in a van, and I need it fixed, I call a mechanic. If I need something built, I can call a carpenter or a handyman. If I need a solar panel installed, I call a RV service facility. Wherever you live, in a house or a vehicle, you will be better off if you learn to do your own repairs or maintenance, but if you can't, you keep living in the house or vehicle and hire someone to do the repair for you. Here are places you can go to find someone to help you convert your van, or even do it for you:

1-Auto mechanic:

Most of the conversion requires a RV tech, but there are a few things a mechanic can do during the conversion. For example, any mechanic should be able to install a solenoid and hook it up to the starting battery and then run it to the house battery in the back of the van. That will charge your house battery every time you drive your car.

2-Handyman:

If you have found a van design you like, but you don't have the time or skill to build it yourself, any decent handyman should be able to build it for you. The best way to do it is ask your friends and neighbors if they have a handyman they recommend. The next step is to print out pictures from the website (right click on the picture and a menu will pop up asking for a location to save it to and allowing you to give it a name, save it to your hard disk). Print the pictures out and take them to the handyman and show them to him.

He should easily be able to visualize what you want and adopt them to fit in your van.

3-Mobile RV repairman:

You might think you should go to a RV Sales and Service Center to get things like your solar panels installed, but my experience has been they are so overpriced, they should be your last choice. I suggest you try to find an independent serviceman if at all possible. The first place to look is in the Yellow Pages of your area. If you don't find someone there, then you should find the RV Parks in your area and either call them or go in person and ask if they know of a mobile RV serviceman. Chances are there is one who is in the RV Park on a regular basis. He may even have a flyer up on the Office bulletin-board. Get his phone number and give him a call.

10-Build a Bed: Getting a good night's sleep is so important to your mental and physical health (plus the need for organization) that if at all possible, I strongly suggest you build your bed before you move in, even if you have to hire a handyman to build it. I have a friend who built her bed out of three end ta-bles she found at Ikea (they cost her $7 each!). They fit perfectly across the back of her van. She went to

Home Depot and had them cut a piece of plywood to fit and just laid it on top of the coffee tables. It has worked perfectly for many years now.

There are a number of ways to build a more permanent bed. The simplest is with 2x4 lumber and plywood. Another is to use sheet metal screws and screw angle iron into the walls of the van and run 2x4s and plywood across. I usually put legs in the middle of the bed for extra strength so it won't sag. Measure your plastic totes so the leg doesn't interfere with getting the maximum number of them under the bed. You are going to need a mattress. Here are some options to finding a mattress:

1-Build the bed to fit a standard size mattress.

2-Find a futon mattress that fits.

3-Find a fabric and foam store in the Yellow Pages. Have them cut a foam pad to the exact size of your bed. You want to buy furniture grade foam because the cheaper foam isn't high enough quality. If there isn't a foam store in your area, look for an Upholstery Shop. They will cut a piece of furniture grade foam to your exact measurements.

4-Many places (Wal-Mart or Target for example) sell memory foam toppers in various sizes and

widths. You can buy one of those and cut it to fit. Memory foam gets hard when it's cold so I suggest you cover it with at least an inch of regular foam.

STEALTH PARKING IN THE CITY:

Finally, you've found the right vehicle and done the basics to be able to live in it. Now where are you going to park? For most people, their first night sleeping in a van is so far out of their comfort zone, it can be very difficult. Your fear will probably magnify every sound (and there are a lot of them) and you may not get much sleep. When you wake up in the morning, you will be disoriented and wonder where you are.

Believe me, I am speaking from experience, I will never forget my first night in a van. I was going through a divorce and was already at a very low point in my life. I felt like I had hit rock-bottom and my life was a failure. I literally cried myself to sleep that night.

I wish I could tell you it gets easier very quickly, but for most people it doesn't. It took me a week before I got a good night's sleep and for many months and even years I woke up disoriented, wondering where I was. I'm telling you all this so that you will be prepared for the worst and not give up before it gets better. And I promise you it does get better. Within a month or two of moving into my van I fell in love with the lifestyle. I loved the freedom and simplicity it offered me, and hopefully you will too!

Where you are going to park depends on whether you are living in a city, or are a traveling vandweller. Finding a parking place is much more difficult for a city vandweller because many (most?) cities do not want you living in a vehicle, in fact many make it illegal to live in a van or sleep on city streets. Traveling vandwellers have a much easier time of it because there is a great deal of Public Land and truck stops that welcome travelers and campers. First we will look at stealth parking, then later at boondocking in the country.

General Rules of Stealth Parking: As we've said, many cities not only frown on living in a van in their city, it's illegal and they are ready to either chase you away or give you a ticket if they catch you. So to avoid problems with law enforcement we are going to work hard to operate below their radar. **If they don't notice us, they won't hassle us.** We are going to do that by hiding in plain sight and blending in as much as possible. Following these rules will help keep you safe:

1-Don't Draw Attention to Yourself:

If you paint a bulls-eye on your back, don't be surprised if somebody shoots at you! For example, if you drive an old Volkswagen bus painted bright colors you can expect to be hassled by law enforcement on a regular basis. In the same way, if you plaster your van with bumper stickers, you can expect to be hearing lots of knocks on your door at night by a police officer. If you've chosen a vehicle with high stealth, don't ruin it by putting anything on it that will draw attention to you

2-Keep Your Vehicle Clean and Neat:

If your vehicle is an old, dirty, rust-bucket, the police are going to pay special attention to you. You may not be able to do anything about its age, but you can keep it clean and tidy looking. Just washing and waxing it tells authorities you take some pride in yourself. It may be older, but you still take care of it. As you have the money, either buy a nicer, newer van, or upgrade the cosmetics of your current vehicle.

3-Remember, the Police are Not the Enemy:

It's very easy to fall into the trap of thinking the Police are the enemy. But that is just lazy thinking. The great majority of law enforcement officers are doing their very best in a difficult job to protect and serve their community. Of course there may be a few bad apples, but they are few and far between. Let me make a strange suggestion. When you have decided to live in your van, visit your local police department and tell them you are being forced to live in a van and is it possible to do that in their city. A surprising number of communities are setting aside an area of town for car and vandwellers to live in. During these hard economic times, some Police Departments are sympathetic towards the newly homeless and do what they can to watch over them.

What's the worst thing that can happen by approaching the police? They tell you that living in your van is illegal and warn you not to do it. That knowledge is very helpful to you. First, knowing that may be incentive for you to move to a friendlier town. Second, if you can't leave, at least you know exactly what you are up against and can live with maximum stealth and plan on a hostile environment. So whether going to the police brings good or bad news, you still come out ahead.

4-Arrive at Your Sleep-Place Late, and Leave Early:

Once you have decided where you are going to sleep, you want to spend the minimum amount of time there. Let's assume you are working at a job and you get off work at 5: 00 pm and you are going to sleep in the parking lot of a local 24-hour Safeway grocery store. You don't want to get to the Safeway until the very last minute. So if you are going to sleep at 11: 00 pm, get to the Safeway at 10: 55 pm, settle in, and go to bed and sleep. As soon as you wake up, get in the driver's seat and drive away. Stop at a convenience store to go in and use their restroom and get cleaned up for the morning. The less time you are at the Safeway, the less likely you are to draw attention to yourself and get thrown out.

So where are you going to spend your evening from 5: 00 pm when you get off work and 11: 00 pm when you go to bed? Anywhere but at Safeway! One good choice is a Barnes and Nobles Bookstore where you can go in and read. Another good choice is a gym where you work out and shower. Many places have a free WIFI hotspot where you can get online and surf the Net. Nearly all cities have broadcast television stations you can pick up with an antenna. So you go park anywhere, put out your antenna and watch TV. Just before bedtime, you take down the antenna, leave there, go to the Safeway, and go to bed.

5-Have Your Story Ready:

No matter how careful you are, there is always the possibility of being rousted in the middle of the night and being asked why you are there. In my experience and in the experiences of most people I have talked to, the majority of times the Officer is not there to hassle you, he is there to check on your safety. No matter what he wants, it is very important that you be respectful and polite.

It will make your interaction go better if you have a story ready to go. If you are in a Walmart parking lot, where are you coming from and where are you on your way to? If you are in the parking lot of a hospital, who are you there to visit? If you are outside an auto repair shop, what's wrong with your car? If the Officer listens to your story and says you have to leave, ask him where you can go instead. If you've been respectful, chances are very good he will offer a suggestion.

6-Use Camouflage:

There are two things that can help hide the fact you are living in a cargo van: 1) A magnetic sign advertising you as some type of a business. A sign that says you are in the heating and plumbing business is an especially good idea. If you are parked in front of either a business or residence a Police Officer driving by will just think you are on a late night emergency call. 2)A ladder rack with a ladder on it makes you look more like a genuine business van. I strongly recommend you cover the ladder rack with plywood which will put the roof in the shade all day keeping the van cooler. It also gives you a place to mount a solar panel without having to drill holes in your roof. Put the solar panel in the middle and the ladders on the outside and they will hide the panel from view, increasing your stealth.

Where to Park: If you park in the same spot all the time, you run the risk of drawing attention to yourself. So to avoid problems with the police you need to have enough parking places that you can rotate among them. Ideally you will have at least seven places so you are only in the same place once a week.

1-A 24-Hour Grocery Store:

By far my favorite sleeping area is in a 24 hour grocery store. I worked on the night, stocking crew of a Safeway Grocery Store for decades, and I can assure you no one inside the store at night knows who is sleeping in a van in the parking lot or even cares. Generally the employees all park in the same area, all you need to do is park somewhere near them and no one will bother you.

All-night grocery stores do have the disadvantage of being noisy with car doors slamming and people talking at all hours of the night.

2-A 24-Hour Restaurants:

Many restaurants, like Denneys, stay open 24 hours, and they also are an excellent choice for all the same reasons as 24-Hour grocery stores.

3-Residential Areas:

There are many different types of residential areas, but by far the best is an area with multiple, large apartment buildings, and the more the better. When you have that many people living in a small area, nobody can keep track of their neighbors, their neighbors guests, or what they drive. Another van on the street won't draw any attention. However, they have the drawback of being noisy, with lots of people coming and going at all hours of the night.

4-Big Box Stores (Wal-Mart):

When we talk about where to spend the night in a van or RV, most people think of Wal-Mart first. And that is its biggest drawback: the Police and security expect people to sleep in their parking lots. In my experience, if a city passes laws prohibiting Overnight Parking there will be strict enforcement at a Wal-Mart and probably none at any other stores. So if you try to sleep in a Wal-Mart parking lot, you will be rousted in the middle of the night, but if you drive across the street and sleep in a Home Depot or Kmart parking lot, you will be left alone. That kind of selective enforcement is very common. So my suggestion to you is to park anywhere but at Wal-Mart. Here are some alternatives: Sam's Club, Target, Costco, Home Depot, Lowes, Kmart, Sears, JC Penney, and many others.

5-Mall Parking Lot:

One of the very best places to park is a strip mall parking lot with many different buildings clustered around the lot. You can park between the buildings and no one will know which building you are in. This works extremely well if one or more of the businesses are 24 hours. A mall in my town had a convenience store on one corner. It was easy to park between the convenience store and the mall and no one knew which one I was in. It was a little noisy at night, but I never had a problem with security or the Police.

6-Auto Repair Shops:

Nearly all mechanics shops have numerous cars parked around it in various stages of repair. Many times you can park on the street in the area and look like you are waiting for a repair. Sometimes all the cars are inside a fenced area and then the risk of getting locked in is so great, you shouldn't park there. If you are approached at night (which is very unlikely) all you need to do is tell them you were having problems with your car and you are waiting for the shop to open in the morning.

7-Hospitals:

Sometimes hospitals are great places to sleep, and sometimes they aren't, it all depends on their level of security. Frequently they have such a high level of security that it is impractical to sleep there. Other times they have lax security and they work great. There is no real problem with trying it one night and finding out. The worse that probably will happen is they ask you to leave.

8-Motels:

Motels are like hospitals in that sometimes they have such tight security you can't sleep in their lot while others are very loose and it is a great place to park. Ideally they will have a store or restaurant on the corner of their lot. If so you can park in-between them and no one will know which you are in.

9-Churches:

The problem with parking in a church parking lot is that people in the area and from the church know who should be in their lot, and who shouldn't be. So you will stand out if you park there. This is one of those times you would be better off going into the office on a weekday and asking if it would be okay for you to sleep there. Chances are pretty good they will say yes.

10-Autos For Sale:

In many towns there is a corner of a large parking lot where there are numerous cars parked with "For Sale" signs in their windshields. It isn't a used car lot, it is just a corner where people have learned they can try to sell their cars. It works pretty well for you to carry a "For Sale" sign and park among the other cars with a sign in your window. However, you run the risk of being there when the police or the owner of the lot decides to impound all the cars parked their illegally. The safest thing is to watch it long enough to be pretty sure that isn't going to happen. But you can never be 100% certain.

11-Industrial Complex:

You can go to any large Industrial complex like a power house, chemical plant, refinery, mine or mill and blend in by parking in the construction parking lots. I have a friend who has worked in a lot of plants and everyone he ever worked in had separate parking lots. One lot will require you to go through security or have a sticker on your windshield. This lot is usually for the plant employees only. The other lot is for the temporary tradesmen (iron-workers, boiler-makers, millwrights, labors, electricians). Many times during a large shutdown there could be hundreds of workers working around the clock. He has slept in these lots before with no problem. The parking lots are usually well lit and there is security nearby. And best of all no one knows who is who and you don't have to pass through security to park in the construction lots. Now obviously this isn't going to work all the time as construction isn't always going on in that particular plant. One thing about this option is that there is no shortage of these types of plants around. They are in cities and out in the country. Finding a plant to park at is fairly easy, just look for smoke stacks.

BOONDOCKING ON PUBLIC LAND:

After my divorce forced me into living in a van, I continued to live in the city because that is where my kids and my job were. In nearly every way my life went on much as it had before, except I lived in a van instead of a house. A few years later, after my kids had grown up and left home, I had the choice to live where I wanted. So I took early retirement which gave me a small pension to live on

Since I had always loved camping and being in the outdoors, the choice was very simple for me, I wanted to live on Public Land. So the very first thing I did was to move to the Southwestern states because I knew there was a huge amount of BLM desert land and National Forest land I could live on free. In the last 4 years I've paid $10 for camping and spent virtually every night in the backcountry. I can't tell you how much I enjoy waking up every morning and stepping out of my tiny home into a beautiful desert or Forest. I may have a tiny home, but I have an unbelievably enormous backyard!

I know living in the backcountry isn't for everybody, if it isn't for you, just skip ahead to the next section. Most of us grew up in cities and never spent any time camping. If that is you, then you would probably feel odd trying to live on Public Land. I've invited new vandwellers out here and they often tell me the quietness and slow pace of the woods is very difficult for them. I always respond by telling them that nature has a magical ability to change us if we will allow it. Sometimes the process is slow and sometimes it is fast, but eventually it always happens if given the time.

Four Reasons You Should Live On Public Land:

1-You can live on very little money:
Of course you aren't paying for a home, but you don't do that when you live in the city either. The reason you can spend less money in the backcountry is that there is nothing to spend it on!! On many occasions I have set up camp and not left it to go into town for a week or two, or even more. That means I am not burning any gas or shopping at any stores. It literally is impossible for me to spend money. Simply being away from the strangle-hold of the true god of this world, Consumerism, means I won't spend much money. One tip I can offer you is that the small mountain and desert towns near where I camp all have very expensive prices. So I try to make a once-a-month, (or every other month) trip to the big city where I stock up on supplies at very low prices. Perishables I buy locally.

2-It is Extremely Good for you Physically.
Every single person that I know who lives this way has lost weight and regained energy. When you live in nature, you just automatically become more active and that means burning more calories

Most people who boondock have so much extra free time, they develop new hobbies. I walk my dog an hour or two every day and work on my werbsites. Several friends took up crafts like jewelry making or painting. One person I know made it her goal to kayak all 50 states. Another friend became a rock hound, constantly searching for nice gems. Many take up photography, exploring for that next great shot. Those hobbies (and many more) keep their mind and bodies active, improving their health.

3-It Will Work Wonders for Your Mental and Emotional Health:

Think of all the stress that would fall away from you if you didn't live in a city. The traffic, noise and violence will no longer be part of your life. Nature is tremendously calming. In fact I think that is why so many people have trouble adapting to it. Their nervous system is in a constant state of heightened alert in the city, perpetually scanning for danger, and when the danger is gone in the country, they feel lost.

When I lived in the city, my mind was constantly churning with the problem of the day. It might be my job, family, friends, anything. My mind was constantly turning over a problem and chewing on it. Out here there is literally nothing for my mind to work on. My mind is quiet and silent: I am at peace.

4-You'll Make Deep Friendships:

I've covered this before, but I need to mention again that as soon as I left living in the city and started living in the backcountry I suddenly found myself with more friends than I ever had before. I know it is counter-intuitive, but it is totally true for me and for nearly everyone I know who lives out here.

How to Live on Public Land: So we've covered why you should live on Public Land, now let's cover how to. All across the country there are National Forests and BLM land that is open to the public for recreation. I'm sure you are already familiar with the many campgrounds on it, but most of them have a fee (although some are free) so that isn't what I am talking about. What I'm talking about is officially called **"dispersed camping."** In government-speak that means camping throughout the forest or desert in other than official campgrounds. It is available in nearly all Public Lands, National Forest or BLM. You just drive down a legal road, find a nice camp spot and set up camp. How far off the road you are allowed to setup camp changes drastically from area to area, so check with your local Ranger Station to find the local rules.

There are some exceptions. Sometimes dispersed camping is limited or prohibited altogether. Generally that's because the area is close to a large population center or has a very high usage. Other times it is because the land is especially sensitive to damage. In order to protect the land from damage or overuse, dispersed camping is limited.

Generally, I assume an area is open to dispersed camping unless there are signs saying it is closed to camping or you must camp in designated areas only. Again, you will need to check with the local Ranger stations to find out exactly where you can camp in that specific area.

Most Dispersed Camping is limited to 14 days (but sometimes it is 21 days) and then you must move a specified distance to your next camp, generally it is around 20 miles, but not always. In some areas there is strict enforcement of that rule, and in others it is very lax. I've been in Forests where I saw people set up camp on a main road with Rangers driving by every day, and they stayed there all summer, never once did a Ranger ask them to leave. And I've been in areas where the Ranger came by on day 14 and made it very clear you had to leave. You are just going to have to be observant of your area to know which you are in.

I have a friend who tries to get as far from the main roads as he can before he sets up camp. He does that by progressively taking smaller, less maintained roads until he is far off the beaten path. Here is an example of roads he may take:

Main Paved Road=>Minor Paved Road=> Major Maintained Dirt Road=>Minor Dirt Road=>Poorly Maintained, Tiny Dirt Road=>Barely-a-Road Dirt Road=>Set-Up Camp

Now, if you get that far back, chances are you won't see a Ranger the whole time you are camping. My friend will set up camp and spend the whole summer there, but I can't recommend you do that. You will have to decide for yourself the legality and morality of how long you camp in one spot. Whatever you decide, follow Leave No Trace rules and take everything out with you that you take in.

Also, be aware that both the Forest Service and BLM have just made major changes in how many roads you can drive on legally. Be sure to stop by the Ranger Station and get a Motor Vehicle Use Map before you head out or you may find yourself camping illegally and end up getting a fine. Lots of boondockers are complaining about these new rules, but I'm not one of them. I've seen too much Public Land torn-up and trashed by obnoxious ATVers and Jeepers to be sympathetic towards limits on them. I camp on Public Land because I love and treasure it and I don't want to do anything to harm it. If some restrictions on roads will accomplish that, I'm all for it. It's just another example of the tiny minority ruining things for all of us. They are the bad guys, not the Rangers who are enforcing therules.

THE YIN AND YANG OF VANDWELLING:

Next we will look at the basics of daily life for the vandweller. The first thing you'll notice is that it isn't nearly as easy and trouble-free as it was when you lived in a house. In fact sometimes it is downright unpleasant. When you hear that, you may think it is a good reason to not live in a van, but I think it is the best reason youshould live in a van. Facing some discomfort is part of being a living human being. **Only the dead are in a constant state of never feeling uncomfortable**. As far as I am concerned the modern world's obsession with comfort and safety is a form of living death.

A vandweller may feel discomfort, but he also feels elation, and joy. I am a total believer in the principle of Yin and Yang; the idea that everything in life is composed of opposites. But they aren't opposites in the sense of being at war with each other. They are two inseparable parts of one whole that complement and co-create each other. Much like the two sides of one coin; they are opposites but the coin can't exist without both.

For example, without feeling bad, you can't understand feeling good. Without being hot, you can't understand cold. That darkness can't exist without light and life can't exist without death. Without danger and risk, there can't be an appreciation of safety. Modern humans, by trying to avoid all discomfort, guarantee they will never know happiness. Instead, life becomes a living death of boredom, monotony and nothingness.

Human beings are the ultimate example of Yin and Yang. On one hand we are highly evolved, enlightened (and I think spiritual) creatures, and on the other hand we are animals with ancient, base instincts that were once critical for our safety and survival but are now mainly a hindrance.

If you and I are to be happy, we must balance the Yin and Yang of our lives. I firmly believe that vandwelling is one of the best possible ways to do that. I can sit in my van with my computer and feed my higher, evolved self, and then I can poop in a bucket and fight the cold and feed my cave-man self.

RECONNECTING WITH YOUR AUTHENTIC SELF:

For thousands of years humans were able to go to the bathroom and stay clean without indoor plumbing, toilets, showers or hot water. Only very recently has it become so incredibly easy to relieve ourselves indoors and have our waste miraculously whisked away. Never before have humans been able to keep meticulously clean with such ease. Chances are fair that yours and my grandparents or great-grandparents used an outhouse and warmed water on a wood stove to bathe. Modern technology and fossil fuels have combined to make our lives easy beyond their imaginations.

So when I suggest to you that you may have to rough it by pooping in a bucket and bathing with wet wipes and wash clothes you probably think I am asking too much of you. But as you consider the possibility, bear in mind that 99% of the humans who ever lived have done just that. In fact even as you read this the majority of people alive right now don't have indoor plumbing. Why should you or I be any different?

In many ways living in a van is getting back to our authentic roots as human beings. It is re-connecting with nature in much the same way our ancestors were connected to nature. Think about the normal American life. You live in a heated, air conditioned house that is sealed up so tight that no part of the outside (nature) can get in to make your life in any way unpleasant. You are insulated from heat, cold, wind, bugs, noise, dirt and anything else uncomfortable about the earth. It is a life alienated from, and at war with, nature.

Unfortunately, it has also resulted in our becoming more and more alienated from one another. Humans have always been pack animals. Later, as we evolved into Homo Sapiens, we lived in tribes. Our lives depended on each other, and to be removed from the tribe was a death sentence. But as we became "civilized" our connection with the earth and each other began to break down.

In modern civilization we live next door to people and yet never make any connection with them. Most of us don't know their names and never say anything to them except courtesy greetings. With the internet we have the dubious pleasure of having friends we never lay eyes on. A disconnection with nature inevitably leads to a disconnection with those around us and with our true selves.

Whether you like it or not, living in a van leads to a life much closer to nature. But more than that, it will also lead to a deep healing of our souls. When you live in a van, you feel nature. When it is hot out, you get hot. When it is cold, you get cold. When the wind blows, the van rocks. When the bugs are bad, you get bitten. When a Raven lands on the roof in the morning, you hear the clacking of his claws. When you poop, and pee you are going to have to deal with it. And sometimes you are not going to be 100% spotlessly clean.

Being uncomfortable is inevitable for a vandweller, but that doesn't mean we don't want to avoid it as much as possible. Next we will look at how to live our daily lives while minimizing out discomfort and maximizing our happiness.

HOW TO GO TO THE BATHROOM:

One thing we all have in common is that we all pee and poop. No one is so rich, powerful or enlightened that he doesn't have to urinate and defecate. Wiping our butt is the great equalizer. I think there is a great lesson in humility in that. I may be smarter than my dog (at least I hope I am) but pooping is much easier for him than it is for me. Going to the bathroom in a van or vehicle is more difficult, but it is only a minor problem and easily overcome. Here are some solutions:

1-Use Public Restrooms:

If you are in a city this is a fairly easy solution. Nearly everywhere you go in a city there are public restrooms you can use. I try to buy something from the store to repay them, but sometimes that just isn't possible. However, it is very inconvenient to have to run out in the middle of the night to answer natures call, and sometimes the need to go is so urgent there isn't time to get into a store to use their restroom. As I've gotten older, it seems like the time from becoming aware of the need to go and having to go **RIGHT NOW**, has become very narrow. For those times, even city dwellers need to be able to go in the van. If you live in the country, there aren't as many public restrooms, but as we will see, there are other good solutions.

2-Using a Pee Pot:

For as long as people have lived in buildings they have been using chamber pots. For most of human history there were no artificial lights and there were predators prowling around outside looking for an easy dinner (which humans are). Beyond that if the weather was cold or rainy, who wanted to go outside in that? So in every way it was better to urinate or defecate inside. Since for nearly all that time there was no indoor plumbing, people just used a container inside the building and then disposed of it the next day, when it was light and safe. Since vandwelling is very much a return to our natural roots, we will also learn to go in a container

3-Separating Solids and Liquids:

It is very helpful that you not urinate and defecate into the same container. Either one is easy to deal with by themselves, but together they become a hassle. It will take some training on your part to keep them separated, but it isn't difficult. You pee in one pot, and poop in another. Urine is easy to deal with it, so we will talk about it first.

4-Pee Pots:

Peeing in a container is very easy for men. In fact the majority of men have peed in a container sometime in their life. Perhaps you were driving and just couldn't find a place to go or didn't have time to stop, so you peed in a coke bottle or whatever else was handy. Well, that is basically all we are talking about, finding a container and peeing in it. One of the best containers is a one quart sport water bottle (like a Nalgene) that seals tight. Ideally it will a fairly wide-mouth and should be yellow so no one will know it has pee in it. Carrying a water bottle has become commonplace anymore, so after you use it, you can take it into a public restroom and dispose of it down the toilet and no one will know what you are doing. It's important that you keep the bottle rinsed out or it will start to smell, so after putting the urine in the toilet, fill it half full with water in the bathroom, put some soap in it, shake it up, and flush the rinse water down the toilet. In the country you just take it a safe distance from camp and dump it. A water bottle is ideal, but any fairly wide-mouth container with a lid will work.

5-Urinals for Women:

As we all know, going to the bathroom is a little more complex for women than for men, but there are solutions for them for as well. One is the use of a urinal for women, which essentially is a funnel designed for a woman's anatomy to urinate into a wide-mouthed container. Brand names change on these all the time, so I suggest you do a Google search on "women's urinal" or searching for the same on Amazon.com. Another solution is to find a very wide-mouthed container and use it directly. An example is a large coffee can with a plastic lid, or a 2 ½ gallon ice cream container with a plastic lid. They are so large no funnel is needed; you just pee directly into them. The plastic lid prevents spills.

6-Peeing in the Great Outdoors:

Chances are we have all done this sometime. You just pick a bush or tree that is private and do your thing. If you are going to be camped in the same place for very long, you want to go fairly far away from camp (30 yards) and change your location every day. If you continually go in the same place you will harm the foliage and it will start to smell. I speak from experience.

7-Pooping in a Five Gallon Bucket:

In the 10 years I have lived in a vehicle, I have always had a 5 gallon bucket to poop in. The reason I like them is they are cheap ($4 at Home Depot), light, multi-use, easy, and portable. Using one is very simple. I use two 13 gallon trash sacks to line the bucket, poop in it, wrap it up in the first sack and then wrap that in the second sack. Then I throw it away in a trash can. Many people tell me that throwing it away is very bad. And it may be, but every day tons of baby poop is thrown away in trash cans and the same with dog feces from people walking their dogs. Since only a tiny number of people live in their vans, I think the net effect is very minor. Some people use kitty litter, or sawdust to get multiple uses out of the sacks. But I prefer to make it a one-time use, wrap it up, and throw it away.

8-Making the Bucket Comfortable:

If you have ever sat on the top of a 5 gallon bucket, you know it is uncomfortable. I know of three solutions: 1) Buy a cheap toilet seat at

Home Depot and put it on top of the bucket. Next trace a circle around the top of the bucket with a Magic Marker. Screw some small scraps of wood around the circle you traced so that when you set the seat on top of the bucket, it won't slide around. 2) Go to Home Depot and buy a piece of pipe insulation. This is a round piece of insulation that is hollow to wrap around pipes so they don't freeze. It has a slit the length of it to allow you to push it over the pipe. To make a toilet it seat out of it, you spread the slit apart and push it down over the 5 gallon bucket. Once it goes around the bucket cut the excess off and duct tape it to the bucket. I've done this and had it last for many years. 3) There is a commercial product called a Luggable Loo. It is designed to snap on top of a 5 gallon bucket and turn it into toilet. Do a Google or amazon.com search on it.

9-Porta-Potti:

If the other solutions just seem too crude, you may like a Porta Potti instead. There are two kinds, the first is just a single piece and is nothing more than a fancy 5 gallon bucket, Don't buy one of those, they are terrible and a huge waste of money. The other kind has two parts. The top holds water to flush with and the bottom is a holding tank that holds the flush water and your waste. These are very comfortable, sanitary and work very well. To use it, first you fill the top part with water and then put some deodorant designed for Porta Pottis in the bottom part. Next you have a bowel movement in it and "flush" it with rinse water, and wait till it fills up. I have a friend who uses one and he is able to go two weeks before he has to dump it. Once the holding tank is full, you separate the top from the bottom part and take the bottom part to a toilet or dump station. The Porta Potti comes with a hose that attaches to the side of the holding tank. You put the bottom of the hose down the toilet (or dump station) and open the valve on the porta potti and its contents go right down the toilet. No muss, no fuss. Then you refill the top part with water and add deodorant to the bottom, and you are all done. You can dump them in any public toilet.

HOW TO SHOWER AND STAY CLEAN:

There is an old saying you are probably familiar with that says that "Cleanliness is next to Godliness." Without being aware of it, most of us have adopted that as a motto for our lives. But think about its full

117

meaning: if cleanliness is next to godliness, then being dirty is demonic and of the devil.

It goes back to the Fundamentalist Christian belief that in the Garden of Eden, Adam and Eve fell into sin and they and the Earth itself became corrupted and are literally fallen from Grace with God. That led to the belief that things of the Earth are evil and things of the spirit are good. We were given the jobs of subduing and hating our bodies (and the earth) and becoming their masters so we could overcome their evil influence over us.

You may be saying to yourself that you aren't affected by that thinking, but having grown up in our culture and society you are probably obsessed with cleanliness. Over the course of your life, how many commercials have you seen for soaps and shampoos? Over and over again, in a thousand different ways you have been told that if you are dirty in even a tiny way, you will become an outcast from your friends, family and society. If you have dandruff, everyone will stare at you and reject you. But if you use "Head and Shoulders," everyone will love you. In our minds, cleanliness is equated with happiness.

Don't misunderstand me, I am not promoting being dirty. In fact just the opposite is true. Dirty people stand out and draw attention to themselves. As a vandweller the last thing you want is to have people noticing you, so keeping your van, clothes and yourself clean is very important. What I am saying is that it is possible to be clean without being obsessed with it.

Probably the question I hear more often than anything else is, "How will I take a shower?" My answer is that staying clean is easy, but taking a shower is quite a bit harder. They aren't the same thing. For thousands of years humans were able to stay clean without indoor plumbing, showers or hot water. Only recently has it become so incredibly easy to stay meticulously clean with such ease. In that brief period of time we have forgotten how to stay clean without indoor plumbing. Next we will take a refresher course in staying clean.

1-Buy a Gym Membership:

The first thing I did when I moved into a van was join a gym. Every day I worked out and took a shower, but you can just go and take a shower if you prefer. Gyms are a simple, easy solution to the problem of staying clean. If you are a traveling vandweller, you should try to look for a gym with nation-wide membership.

2-Spray Bottle and Wash Cloths:

If you have very limited funds or don't live in an area where there is a gym, it is still possible to stay clean with just a simple quart spray bottle and wash cloths. It's as easy as spraying your body with the spray bottle and then scrubbing it with a wet wash cloth. Start from the top and work your way down to the more difficult areas. You can use a bar of soap to get totally clean. Use the spray bottle to rinse with. I've bought lots of cheap spray bottle that broke after just a few uses. The ones I found that lasted the longest came from Home Depot in the cleaning supplies aisle. They have one that has their logo that I've used for six months or longer.

3-Wash Basin:

Nothing could be simpler than pouring some water (hot is nice but cold works just as well) in a small tub and using it to wash yourself. Humans have being doing it for thousands of years. The only thing that's changed is the material the basin is made out of.

4-Wet Wipes:

I like to use wet wipes throughout the day to do light touch ups on the areas of my body that tend to get the dirtiest like the face, neck, hands, arm pits, and crotch. That way they never get really dirty or smelly which makes it easier to clean them at the end of the day with the spray bottle and wash cloths. I buy my wet wipes from Target or Wal-Mart. I buy their brand name. They are in a soft pack with a small lid that snaps closed. I like them because they compact as they get used up. I store them in a 1 gallon Ziploc so they stay moist for many months. I've never had one dry out.

5-Washing Your Hair:

You can fairly easily wash your hair inside the van by leaning over a large basin and pouring water over your head. If you live in the country, it is also easy to just pour water over your head to wash your hair. Many vandwellers have found that going without shampoo makes it easier to wash and rinse their hair, and has also made their hair healthier. Do a Google search on "washing your hair without shampoo" to find lots of information on traditional house dwellers who have discovered the many benefits of not using shampoo. It's also possible to make a slurry of baking soda and water which works extremely well to keep your hair clean very easily.

Another option is to use the no-rinse shampoo that hospitals use for some for their patients. You just work it into your hair and let it dry, no rinsing required.

6-Making Your Own Shower Enclosure:

While it isn't practical to shower outside if you live in the city, if you live in the country, it is quite easy to set up a shower enclosure. If you live in a van you can just open the back doors (or the side doors if they open out) and hang a shower curtain or tarp across the doors. You can use strong magnets or hooks to hold it in place. Stansport is a maker of inexpensive sporting goods that makes a very good shower/toilet tent. It is like a small tent that is shaped just for showers. It costs less than $50, goes up very easily and gives you plenty of privacy. I've left mine set-up in the desert with winds over 50 mph and it withstood them very well. Do a search on 'camp shower enclosure" on Amazon.com or Google for many choices.

A cheaper alternative if you are in the forest is to use rope and tarps strung between trees to make a shower and toilet enclosure. The cheapest and simplest way is to shower outside while wear a bathing suit. Finish cleaning your private areas inside after you are done.

7-How to Have Hot Water:

You don't have to have hot water to stay clean, but let's face-it, it's much more pleasant if you do. The obvious way to make hot water is to put a large pan filled with hot water on your propane stove and warm it up. It works but you will burn quite a bit of propane and it will take a long time. A simple and cheap alternative is to use a solar shower. It is a black bag that generally holds 5 gallons of water. If you set it out in the sun in the morning, you should have 5 gallons of hot water by noon. The bag will have its own shower head, all you need to do is hang the bag above your head and gravity will pull the water down on you to bathe with.

You can make your own by taking 1 gallon water jugs and painting them black and setting them out in the sun. You can then just pour the water over yourself or use a small battery-operated pump to pump it up. One way to get them hotter faster is to take a reflective auto windshield shade and wrap it around the solar bag or water bottles painted black.

Finally, you can buy a propane fired hot water on demand system designed specifically for camping, do a Google or Amazon.com search on "camping propane hot water on demand". Zodi makes a very good system that uses the little green propane bottles to make hot water on demand and includes a small pump to pump the water up to a shower head. You can buy just the pump by itself if you are making your own hot water on your stove. Eco temp makes a much more advanced system for outdoor use that makes much more hot water per minute, but it does not include a pump, you have to buy your own (Shurflow makes the best 12 volt pumps).

HOW TO COOK IN THE VAN:

After I first moved into my box van, I found myself going out to eat very frequently. I hadn't learned how to cook in the van yet, so I ended up eating fast food and at restaurants nearly every meal. I wasn't very happy about that because it was costing me a lot of money and I wasn't eating as healthy as I wanted to. So I decided to learn how to cook in the van. Like we said before, living in a van is very similar to going camping, the only real difference is sleeping on a bed inside the van instead of on a cot in a tent. So cooking for a vandweller is very much like cooking while camping. In fact nearly everything you need you can get at a sporting goods store. Let's look at what you will need:

1-Propane Stove:

I highly recommend that you buy either a Coleman 1-burner or 2-burner propane camping stove. For the money they are surprisingly high quality and reliable. I have used them without any problem for over 10 years. They use the small, one pound, green propane bottles as a propane source. They have the advantage of being universally available and if you buy them at larger stores they are reasonably priced. If you buy them at small, remote, tourist towns they can be very expensive. Some people worry about storing them inside the van, but I have never had a problem with storing a 1 lb. bottle.

2-Cooking Safely in The Van:

Many people are very concerned about the safety of cooking inside the van. And that is not an unreasonable concern. Every camping stove has a decal on it somewhere that warns against using it indoors because of the risk of carbon monoxide poisoning. However, I think the risk is very low, so I have always cooked inside my van. As I am writing this I have lived in a vehicle for well over ten years and I almost always cooked at least one meal inside the vehicle every day of that time. That means I have cooked at least 3,500 meals in a vehicle. In all that time, I have never had a problem. You have to reach your own conclusions whether you think it is safe to cook inside your van, but I can tell you that for me the risk is extremely small and the advantages are very great so I do.

3-Three Safety Rules I Never Violate:

However, there are three safety rules I never violate: 1) I always have a good quality smoke detector and carbon monoxide detector in the van with me. I spend the extra money and buy the ones that are certified for RV use. My life might depend on them so spending a few extra dollars is money well spent. 2) I never use any kind of liquid fuel in my vehicle. Some examples are kerosene, alcohol, white gas or Coleman fuel. I think the risk is just too great. One spill and your van can go up in flames. There are some very high quality stoves designed for use on boats that burn liquid fuels like diesel. While they are safe, they are also expensive and specialized so I don't recommend them. 3) Some people use small specialized woodstoves inside their van for heat, and also to cook on. To me that is just asking for trouble and so I don't do it nor do I recommend that you do it.

4-Refillable Bulk Propane Bottles:

In the long run you can save a lot of money if you buy a bulk, refillable propane bottle like the one that comes with propane barbeques. They hold 20 lbs (which is 5 gallons) of propane. Generally, buying propane in the small green bottles will cost at least 4 times as much as buying the same amount by the gallon. You will need to buy an adaptor hose to be able to connect it to your camping stove. You can buy it at Wal-Mart, most sporting-good stores, or Amazon.com

5-Carrying Propane Bottles:

One problem bulk bottles have is where will you carry them? It is universally accepted that you should not carry or store them inside a vehicle or inside a house. This is another safety rule that I have always broken. Every day of the 10 years I have lived in a vehicle I have had a bulk propane bottle inside with me, usually stored under my bed. I think the risks from having a propane bottle inside the van is so incredibly small, it isn't worth giving it any thought. The danger is that in the event of a severe accident like a roll-over the bottle can go flying and the valve can break off. The way I keep that from happening is storing the bottle under my bed inside a Rubbermaid tote and wrapping extra blankets around it. Stored there it is safe from being thrown around or damaged from any accident.

6-Butane Stoves:

I know several vandwellers who greatly prefer butane stoves instead of propane stoves. I'm not talking about the tiny backpacking stoves, these are about a foot square and come in a fold-up, self-contained case. They have the advantage of being very small and compact. All of them I have seen come with a push-button spark starter which makes starting them very easy. But they also have three major disadvantages: (A) Butane doesn't work below 32 degrees. I use my propane stove to heat my camper in moderately cold temperatures, so this reason alone means I will never own a butane stove. (B) The bottles of butane they burn are expensive and hard to find.(C) You can't hook them up to a bulk tank to save money on the cost of butane

7-Pots and Pans:

You probably have all the pots and pans you need in your house right now. I can cook every kind of meal I want to with a large 2 quart pot and a 10 inch frying pan, but I also carry a small pot to warm up cans of chili, soup and leftovers. The smaller pot is easier to wash afterwards and heats up faster. I prefer cookware with a non-stick lining like Teflon because they don't stick and are easy to clean. But some vandwellers prefer cast iron or stainless steel.

8-Refrigeration:

Cooking for one person is harder than cooking for a couple or family. So I generally cook a larger amount and then save the rest to re-heat as leftovers. That means I need to have a cooler. For the first 7 years I lived in a vehicle I used an Igloo 5-Day Extreme Ice Chest for refrigeration. I did three things that made living with an ice chest easier. (A) The first thing I suggest you do is add extra insulation. I bought a sheet of 2 inch Styrofoam and cut it to fit the top, bottom and sides of the cooler. Then I used Gorilla Glue to glue it to the cooler. That made a huge difference in how long the ice lasted. (B)The second thing

I did was to put a kitty litter tub inside the cooler and I put the ice inside the tub and the food around the outside of the tub. That made my life so much easier. The food didn't float around in the melt water or get ruined by it, and the ice lasted much longer. (C) Finally, I kept the cooler full. The fuller the cooler is, the longer it stays cold. If I have extra room in the cooler, I add more cans of pop or water bottles so it stays full.

The ice chest worked fine but buying ice was expensive and I hated dealing with the ice water. So as soon as I could afford it I bought a small Dometic 12 volt compressor chest cooler. I love it! My food stays cold and I don't have to buy ice. It was expensive (I paid $400 for a 25 quart size) but I calculated that it paid for itself after two years in the savings of not having to buy ice. I have 190 watts of solar panels on my roof and it easily supplies me with all the electricity I need to run the refrigerator and everything else I need.

9-Microwave:

Let's face it, nearly all of us would like to have the amazing convenience of a microwave oven in our van. It isn't easy, but it is possible. The first question you have to ask is where will you get the power to run a microwave? There are three possibilities (A) Shore power (110 volt electricity from an RV park or a house) (B) A 2000 watt generator (or larger). (C) Use an inverter hooked up to a battery bank. Let's look at each of those to see if they might work for you. Shore power is hard to find unless you have the money to pay for a RV Park I've never once spent a night in a RV Park in the last 10 years of vandwelling so that wouldn't work for me. I do have a microwave in my little trailer and I use my 2000 watt Honda Generator to power it. Remember though, I live on public land so I can easily run my generator outside. But when I lived in a city, it was much more difficult. Before you buy a generator and microwave, be sure that you can safely use them if you are in a city.

Finally, I have 190 watts of solar power and a battery bank so I am able to run a microwave off of it. Not just any inverter will work though. Microwaves are very fussy about the quality of power they receive so you must use a Pure Sine Wave inverter for your microwave. They also draw a lot of power so you will need at least a 1500 watt inverter. A 1500 watt Pure Sine Wave inverter is expensive, expect to pay a minimum of $350 for one and probably more. They are also very large, decide where you are going to put it before you buy one.

There is a product called The Wave Box made by Power Hunt. It is a very small, low-powered (425 watts) microwave that can be powered by 110 volt or 12 volt. You don't need an inverter and it is very easy to hook up to your batteries. I've used one and it works fine. Because it is so low-powered it takes longer to cook food, but it all has gotten cooked just fine. My standard test is microwave popcorn. On my 700 watt compact 110 volt microwave it takes a little less than 3 minutes, and on the Wave box it took 7 minutes. I was able to power it from my battery bank with no problem. It's very small but in the tiny space of a van, that is a big positive instead of a negative. The one disadvantage it has is that it's very expensive at $359. However, that is less than the cost of a cheap microwave and a 1500 watt PSW inverter. It also takes up much less room in the van.

10-Assorted Cooking Methods:

There are several other cooking methods that work especially well for vandwellers. But because of limited time and space I am just going to mention them in passing here. You can do a Google search on them if you want more information. **Thermos Cooking** (also known as hay-box cooking): Essentially you bring the food you are cooking to a boil, then transfer it to a Thermos bottle to finish cooking. The advantage is that you save money by using less propane or butane. **Solar Oven:** I have a solar oven and love it. I bake cakes, bread, roasts, stews, meat-loafs and many other things in it. Anything you can make in an oven or crock pot you can make in a solar oven. I have a commercial oven called the Global Sun Oven. It is expensive but works better than any other solar oven. You can save a lot of money by making your own. There are many plans on the Web. **Pressure Cooker:** there are lots of myths out there about pressure cookers that may make you think you would never own one. But that is to your great loss. They work extremely well and are very safe if used properly. Their main advantage is they greatly reduce the cooking time of many foods. Also, they let you use a lower quality (therefore cheaper) cut of meat and the pressure cooking will make it falling-apart tender. **Rocket Stove:** These are a wood cook-stove with a very advanced design. You can cook a meal on just a few thumb-sized twigs. I spend the summer in the National Forests where there is an abundance of dead-and-down wood so these work very well. They should never be used inside the van. A Google search will give you all the information you need on each of these.

HOW TO STAY IN TOUCH:

While I love the freedom of living on wheels, I have to admit it does create some problems. Our society revolves around people living in a stick-and-brick home. Mail, telephone, television and internet all assume you live at a fixed address. If you don't, things become much more difficult. That became especially true after the fall of the Twin Towers on 9-11. The Patriot Act set in motion new rules and regulations that tie our identity to a physical address. For example, if you try to get a Post Office Box, they will ask you for proof of residency which means a utility bill, rent receipt or some kind of physical proof that you live in a stick-n-brick house. If you don't have one, you can't get a P.O. Box.

State Residency: if you move into a van with the intention of traveling, you have the option to choose the state you want to be a resident of. Several factors make some states much cheaper to live in than others: (A) Some states don't have any income tax which can save you a lot of money each year. (B) Every state charges you to renew your vehicle registration every year or every other year. There can easily be as much as a $1000 difference between two different states in the cost of renewing the same vehicle. (C) The cost of vehicle insurance varies greatly from state to state. (D) Some states require a vehicle inspection every year and others don't. The ones that do will cost you more to live in.

One of the things you need in a state is a mail forwarder who will help you become a resident of that state. They will provide you with both a physical address and a mailing address. Most full-time RVers choose one of these four states as their state of residency because they don't have any income tax and they also have mail forwarders (in alphabetical order):

- Florida

- Nevada

- South Dakota

- Texas.

Each has pluses and minuses, but because you will have to actually be in the state at least once to get your driver's license, I think you should make your decision based on geography; which one is closest to where you will spend most of your time. Since I spend nearly all my time in the Southwest, I became a resident of Pahrump, Nevada, and have been very glad I did. I have a regular doctor there so I get yearly checkups and my dog goes to the same vet every year while we are there. There is a real advantage in having your state of residence be somewhere you travel through every year. Next, let's look at how a Mail Forwarding service works.

How to Get Mail: Without a physical address, how are you going to get mail? Your first thought may be to get a United States Postal Service (USPS) Post Office Box (P.O. Box). But like I said earlier, that will require some kind of proof of living in a physical house. So if you are going to get a P.O. Box, do it while you are still living in your house and you can easily provide proof. There is one major problem with the USPS: they won't accept deliveries from UPS (United Parcel Service, the guys with the brown trucks), FedEx, or any other delivery company. Since the great majority of internet retailers use either UPS or FedEx, having a P.O. Box makes ordering off the Internet very difficult.

A much better choice is to get a box at a UPS Store. All you need to open a box with them is two forms of identification. I have used them when I was in one place for a long time, and they do an outstanding job. You have 24 hour access to your box and when they are open you can make copies, get something notarized and send and receive a fax. They will even forward your mail to you if you are traveling. While they do a good job, they have two main disadvantages, (A)they are very expensive, (B) they do not provide you with a residence address. Instead, they give you a Postal Mail Box (PMB) or a Suite Number, which everyone knows is not a residence. A Mail forwarder will cost you less and give you a true residence address.

I use a mail forwarder in Pahrump, NV that does an outstanding job. Let's look at the services she offers: (A) She charges $100 a year which is about the cheapest I've ever seen. (B) She is a retired woman who works out of her home, and she allows me to use her home address as my home address. So my residence address is 1234 Main Street, Pahrump, NV 89041. My mailing address is P.O. Box 5555, Pahrump, NV(neither of those is real). All my mail goes to the P.O. Box and a UPS order goes to 1234 Main Street. Having a physical address is becoming increasingly important in the post-9-11 world. (C) All my mail and packages goes to my mail forwarder and she holds it for me until I call or email her an address where she can forward it to me. But she does much more than just forward my mail. If I ask her to, she will open my mail and scan and email it to me, or call me and read it to me. Since my bank has a branch in Pahrump, she has even offered to receive a check for me, and take it to the bank and deposit it into my account. She charges a small fee for some of these services, and I leave her a yearly deposit to cover the cost of postage when she sends my mail to me.

You can get more information about her services at jbmailroom.com. All of the states I listed above as being the best choices for traveling vandwellers have mail forwarders specifically designed for RVers:

Florida: the Good Samaritan Club is a famous group for RVers and they have a very popular mail forwarding service

Nevada: jbmailroom.com

South Dakota: The state actively pursues Full-Time RVers to make it their home state so many very well-known Mail Forwarders have sprung up to service them:

Texas: Texas is the home of the Escapees RV club, and it has a very popular Mail Forwarding service.

Cell Phone: It is very difficult for me to give you specific advice about a cell phone plan because there are so many options with so many ins-and-outs that I could write a whole book about it and in a week it would all be out-of-date. So let me give you some broad ideas about cell service:

1-Internet Phone Plans (VOIP Voice Over Internet Protocol):

I've never used one of these but I know people who do and they love them. Their main advantages are there low price, cheap long distance and you can use a web cam for live video as you talk. Because of my inexperience, I am going to let you do your own research. I suggest you start with Skype and Google.

2-PrePaid Plan:

There are many of us who use the phone so little that a simple Pre-Paid Plan can be your best choice. You probably will pay more per minute, but because you use so few minutes it will be much less per month. And because you buy minutes as you need them, you don't have to sign up for a long term plan with its fixed monthly payment.

3-Friends and Family plan:

Most of the major cell service providers offer a friends and family plan. In one of these, one member of the family buys a cell plan, and then adds extra lines for each member of the family. Typically, the extra lines are very inexpensive. I am on a Friends and Family Plan with my ex-wife and my line costs $10 per month plus tax. I am one of those people who hates talking on the phone so I use very few minutes per month. A big plus they have is that you can talk to other phones on the Plan for free.

4-Verizon–The Best Cell Provider:

I'm assuming that since you live in a van, you travel quite a bit so the coverage a cell provider offers is very important to you. If that is so, I am going to go out on a limb and strongly urge you to get a plan with Verizon. In the last four years I have been all over the country and spent the great majority of that time in remote, backcountry locations. Nearly everywhere I have gone I get a strong Verizon signal. I use Verizon for my Data plan and ATT for my cell phone and based on my experience I can tell you that Verizon is a thousand times better than ATT. I've heard good things about Sprints service but I know for sure that Verizon is truly outstanding.

5-Cell Time Re-Sellers:

The FCC doesn't want the big cell phone providers to have a monopoly, so they require them to sell large chunks of cell minutes to smaller cell service providers, who then turn around and resell the minutes to their customers. Because they do not own or maintain the cell towers, they can sell the minutes cheaply, which means you can get some very good deals by going through them. I've known people who went with them and were very happy. Just be sure you know whose towers you are going to be connected to. If they are reselling ATT minutes then a traveling vandweller is going to be very disappointed, but if they are using Verizon towers, you will be very pleased with their coverage. Many resellers won't tell you whose tower they use, if that is the case, I wouldn't sign up with them.

6-Data Phones:

Today's smart phones are truly amazing. With a data plan you can connect to the Internet and have an unbelievable amount of entertainment, information and convenience at your fingertips. If you buy a phone that lets you tether your laptop (connect the laptop to the phone with either a cable or by sending a wifi signal) then your phone plan can also be the data plan for your laptop.

7- 3G Versus 4G:

When you buy a cell phone and you may be using it for Internet access, you want to buy the fastest equipment available. As I am writing this, the industry is in the process of switching from 3G to 4G. That means it is moving from the 3rd Generation to the 4th Generation of data equipment. Most of the country is still using 3G so during the switchover some people are going to keep buying 3G phones but that is f very short sighted. The difference in speed is so dramatic that you don't want to be without it and the industry switches over much faster than you might think.

Internet: Although the internet hasn't been around that long, the majority of us have become dependent on it. I for one, couldn't imagine my life without it. So, how can you have internet access when you live in a vehicle?

1-Internet by Cell Data Providers:

As you must know, all the cell phone providers also offer data access by cell phone signal. You can get a data plan for your cell phone, or you can get a data plan that works just on your laptop and doesn't have a voice plan at all. It has the advantage of being cheaper. Since I have a friend and family plan for my cell phone, I have a data only plan for my laptop.

There are two ways to get the signal into your laptop: A) MIFI, this is a credit card sized device that receives the cell data signal and rebroadcasts it as up to five WIFI signals. That means that up to five other devices can use that data signal. For example, I can have my laptop, Kindle E-reader and Apple iPad connected at the same time and still invite two friends to use it as well. I am paying $50 a month for 5 Gigs of data, but they also have a $80 a month plan for 10 Gigs. B) Another device to get data into your laptop is a Data Stick. It is used for only one laptop at a time and most often connects by the USB port of your laptop, but you can also get them that slide into a slot in your laptop. Both of these work well, but I think the MIFI is a much better choice because it offers you a lot more flexibility.

2-Use Free WIFI Hotspots:

All across the country there are businesses that offer free WIFI in order to get customers to come to their place of business. Usually it is a very fast internet connection. I know many vandwellers who are on such a tight budget that they get all their access that way and are very satisfied with it. There are a couple of problems with it. First, it is not completely secure, it can be hacked and your data can be captured. Second, there isn't always free WIFI nearby, you may have to drive some distance to find it and burn the extra gas or do without the internet.

Banking: If you are a traveling vandweller, how are you going to do your banking? For me the answer was simple, I opened an account with Bank of America because they are truly a nationwide bank with local branches in nearly every state. I have never had a problem with finding either a local branch or a Bank of America ATM. If you have an automatic deposit you can get free checking with them or you can open an E-account that is internet only and is also free. Other people use Credit Unions because of their superior customer service, others prefer internet only banks.

Whichever you choose, be sure to take advantage of automatic deposit of your income and their bill-pay services. Also a Debit card offers the ultimate in convenience. You can use it to order from the internet, make a deposit or get cash from an ATM. Best of all, even if there isn't a local branch close to you, you can use it to pay at a store and then get cash back.

HOW TO HAVE ELECTRICAL POWER:

No matter how simple a life you want to live in your new vehicle home, you are going to need some electrical power. For example you probably want some lights at night and you will want to recharge your laptop or camera. Maybe you want to watch TV or DVDs. In the heat of summer, how will you run a fan? In the cool of winter, how can you power a 12 volt blanket? These are pretty important questions.

After living in my van for a week without power, I knew I had to have it. I like to watch TV and DVD's. I want to be connected to the web via my laptop. I like the convenience of a microwave. So I found a way to have electricity in my box van. There are several ways to do this. We'll start with the easiest, cheapest and simplest and move onto the more expensive and difficult.

Use the car starting battery. While this works, it is not a good idea. You just use the starting battery of your car to run your house needs. Your car probably has a cigarette lighter. Since many 12 volt items come with a plug that goes into the cigarette lighter all you have to do is plug it in and it is running off your car battery. For 110 volt items, you can buy something called an inverter. This allows your 110 volt items to be powered by your car's 12 volt battery. Inverters can be bought for $20-$40 at Wal-Mart. You plug the inverter into your cigarette lighter and then plug your laptop, TV, or battery charger into it. This works fine as long as you are driving, or running your car often.

The problem is that the starting battery in a car is not designed to be discharged and recharged. It should be left nearly full all the time; otherwise it will lose its ability to hold any charge. So if you are parked overnight watching a couple of movies and running your laptop, he next morning your battery will probably be dead and your van won't start. Very inconvenient! Do that a few times and you will be buying a new battery. Very expensive! While this is cheap and easy, it is also the riskiest way to get power. There are better ways.

Buy a Backup Battery Jumper. These are small self-contained batteries with attached jumper cables.

They are intended to be carried in your trunk and jump-start your car if your battery dies. You can buy them with built in tire inflators, lights, and even inverters to run 110 volt items. Nearly all come with an outlet to allow you to plug cigarette lighter items in. Make sure you get one that can be charged from your car's cigarette lighter so you can recharge it while you drive. These have the advantage of providing you with power, and they won't leave you stranded with a dead battery. However, their batteries aren't very good: they are small, will run down quickly with use, and will fail after a few discharges and recharges. So they really aren't a good answer either.

Install a Second Deep Cycle Battery. Your vehicle already has a starting battery under its hood, but we aren't talking about that. We are going to install a second battery back in your living area to use to run your electrical items. It is commonly called a "house" battery because it is being used to run your household items. You will probably be tempted to buy a cheap starting battery to use as your house battery but you want to buy a deep cycle battery instead. Starting batteries are designed to be discharged at most 6-10 times, while a deep cycle battery is designed to be discharged hundreds, or even thousands of times. This solution is by the far the best, so we'll spend a lot of time explaining how to do it.

1-Which Battery to Buy: Marine, Golf Cart or 12 Volt Deep Cycle?

You have three choices of battery type to buy: marine, golf cart, or 12 volt deep cycle. They are all deep cycle batteries, but they vary greatly in price and quality.

A) Marine Batteries: are a hybrid battery that is designed to both start an engine and be discharged multiple times. Like most dual-purpose items, they do two things reasonably well, but don't do either thing extremely well.

B) Golf Cart Batteries: are designed to be used in golf carts and deeply discharged on a daily basis. They are 6 volt batteries so they have to be bought in pairs and wired in series.

C) 12 Volt Deep Cycle Batteries: are designed to be 12 volt and deeply discharged. Unlike golf cart batteries, they can be bought and used one at a time.

Which one of these you buy is going to be decided mostly by your budget. You can buy a cheap marine battery at Wal-Mart for $80, or you can pay $160 for a pair of golf cart batteries from Sam's Club. If you only have $80 then your decision is made, you can't beat the Wal-Mart price. If you buy two of the Wal-Mart batteries, they will have the same capacity as the two golf cart batteries, so which is better?

The first few years they would be about the same. But after that the difference in quality will become obvious. The golf cart batteries are true deep cycle and will last much longer. A company named Trojan makes some of the very best golf cart and deep cycle batteries. Their T105 costs about $130 each. A pair will cost $260 and give you 225 Ah of storage. They are better batteries and will last longer so it may be money well spent

2- Flooded Wet Cell or AGM?

So far we have only talked about traditional flooded wet cell batteries which means they have caps on top and you need to check them every month or so and be sure they have enough water left in them. Not only do they have to be checked for water level periodically, they also vent hydrogen, which is a very dangerous and explosive gas.

There is a new type of battery out now called AGM (Absorbent Glass Matt). They have the advantage that they are sealed, so that they don't vent water or hydrogen so they are zero maintenance and zero risk. You can also store them on their side, or even upside-down, making it easier to find a place for them. In every way it is a better battery but they will cost double or triple the cost of a flooded cell battery, however, their advantages may be worth it to you. The key to deciding which is best for you is deciding where you are going to locate your house battery.

3-Where Will I Carry It?

If you are living in a car, then you don't have much room for a battery bank. Whatever you drive, you must also be aware of weight since the more weight you carry, the harder your engine works, and the less mpg you get. If you have an AGM battery, you can put it anywhere it will fit, even on its side since it can't leak. Maybe you can fit it on its side underneath the driver's seat, or if you are alone, you can put them on the floorboards in front of the passenger seat. It's a different story with regular flooded wet cells. They must be maintained regularly by keeping them full of water and cleaned off. They also vent hydrogen gas which is very corrosive, toxic and explosive. Ideally they will not be in your living area.

So where can you put 60-120 lbs of battery? To be honest with you, I lived in a box van for 6 years with a wet-cell battery under my bed without any problem. Was it dangerous? Everyone tells me it was, but I never had any problem. I can't recommend you do it, I can only report my experience which is that the risk is greatly exaggerated. You can always buy or build a battery box and vent it to the outside if you are concerned about them venting.

In my current home I have a pair of AGM Golf Cart batteries under my bed, and I am extremely happy with them. I don't have to worry about maintaining them or wonder if they are venting hydrogen. However, they cost me $250 each ($500 for the pair) and many people can't afford that much.

I was honest with myself and realized I neglected my wet-cell batteries, so they never lasted very long. I decided that spending the extra money on a battery that didn't need to be maintained was probably going to cost me less in the long run, so I spent the extra money on AGM batteries. They are such a great battery that they came with a 7 year warranty, if they last that long (and I think they will) they will cost me less per year than cheaper batteries that last less than half as long.

4-Charging the Battery from the Car alternator:

Now that you know which battery to buy and where to put it, we have to decide how to keep it charged. We have a built in source of electricity in our car's alternator, so let's tap into it. It isn't as hard as it may sound. You need a cable long enough to go from your cars battery to your house battery. To measure this, tie one end of a string to the positive post of your car battery and wind it down, along the frame, and up to where the battery will be. Measure the string and this is how long your cable needs to be.

Your town or a town nearby probably has a battery store or auto-electric shop which will custom make a cable for you. Tell them the length you need and the size. With cables, the smaller the number, the bigger the physical size of the cable. A size 0 cable should be big enough for simply charging the battery. Ask your retailer. They will also put the ends on for you.

You will probably need to drill at least a half inch hole through the floor to get the cable in. Be sure and put a rubber grommet in the hole so the sharp metal doesn't wear the rubber off the cable causing a short.

Your house battery needs to be grounded. Grounds are very important, so take your time and do it right. The best way is to run a 4 gauge wire from the negative of your house battery, through the hole you just drilled and to the frame of the vehicle. Look around and find a hole in the frame. I was lucky and found a hole close by. If you can't find a hole, look for a bolt to take off and use it for a ground. If you can't find anything, drill a new hole. Scrub the area around the connection with a screwdriver, knife or sand paper until you have shiny new metal. Then I put on a thin layer of Vaseline to keep rust from forming. You may be tempted to go directly to the body because it's so easy, but there isn't enough metal mass to be an adequate ground. That's because bodies are attached to the frame with a rubber gasket to give a better ride.

Next, attach the cable ends to the positive pole of the house and starting battery and you are in business! Your house battery is being charged by your car alternator. However, you still have a problem, if you use too much juice in your house battery; it pulls whatever is needed from the starter battery. If it draws too much, it won't start the car and you are stranded. Do that a few times and we are buying a new starting battery. Here are some solutions to this problem.

5-Installing a Battery Selector Switch:

The first and simplest is a battery selector switch. You attach the cable from the starting battery to this switch and run a cable from the switch to the house battery. When you are going to be using the house battery, you turn the switch to **"Off"**. This isolates the house battery from the starting battery so it can't draw it down. The next day, when you are done camping and about to drive off, turn the switch to **"On"** and now the two batteries are connected again and the house battery is being recharged. Simple and easy.

But what if you forget to turn the switch off? You run the risk of running your starting battery down and being stranded. One way around this is replace your starting battery with a marine starting battery which will not be damaged if you forget to turn the switch off. And carry a jumper battery as discussed earlier. But there is a better solution that won't leave you stranded at all.

6-Installing a Continuous Duty Solenoid:

The next solution is a little more complex but solves all of our problems by using a continuous duty solenoid between the two batteries. A good auto store will sell these or you can Google "continuous duty solenoid" and order one over the net. Don't buy an intermittent duty solenoid, it won't last. It must say "continuous duty".

Once you have it, you mount it to the firewall of your vehicle. A cable runs from the starting battery positive post to one of the large studs on the solenoid. A cable leaves the other large post and runs back to the positive post of your house battery.

On some solenoids there will be two smaller posts. One is for a ground to the frame; the other is to a hot wire in the vehicle wiring harness. Some solenoids are self-grounding, so they only have one of the small posts. The screws that secure it to the firewall act as the ground. If that is what you have, take extra care to have a good clean connection for the ground. If there is paint on the fender or firewall where you are attaching the solenoid, you must scrap the paint off so that you have a clean metal-to-metal connection. That thin layer of paint will prevent a good ground.

Whether you have one or two smaller posts, you must run a wire to the vehicle wiring harness, which isn't as hard as it sounds. Wherever you splice in, it must be after the ignition, so that when you turn the key off, power is turned off to the solenoid as well. A good, easy place for this is the power to the radio since we know that when you turn off the key, the radio losses power and turns off.

The way it works is that when you turn on the key, power goes to the solenoid which activates a magnet inside it. The magnet lifts a bar which makes a connection between the two large posts, allowing charging current to flow from the starting battery to the house battery. When you turn the key off, current no longer flows to the solenoid, the magnet turns off, the bar falls and there is no longer a connection between house and starting battery. That means that if the engine is running, the house battery is being charged, and if it is off, the house battery can not run down the starting battery. The best of both worlds! Absolutely no drawbacks.

7-Installing a Battery Isolator:

Another solution, and by far the most common, is using a battery isolator. These are commonly available at any auto parts or RV store. Because these have a half volt drop between the house and starting battery, I don't recommend them. Therefore, I am not going to cover them very much. Just follow the instructions that come with them if you want to use one.

8-Charging the Battery from a Generator:

For several reasons I won't go into, just charging off the alternator won't be adequate to keep your battery fully charged. A great answer is a generator. You may think a generator isn't for you because of their many problems: A) there isn't room in your car/van/RV for it, B) they are too heavy to lift in and out and too hard to start, C) when they are running, they are so loud they drive you crazy, D) plus, they burn too much gas.

All of that is true of past models of generators, but fortunately none of it is true of a new generation of Honda and Yamaha generators. They are tiny, light, quiet, start easily and sip gas. And they will run very close to forever. You may think I am exaggerating but seeing is believing. Visit a Honda or Yamaha dealer and be amazed how practical they are for car/van/RV living.

Their one problem is that they are fairly expensive. You can get the 1000 watt model for about $700 over the net. If you have the money, they are worth it. A 2000 model is about $950 but it has enough power to run a microwave, portable electric heater, or small portable or window Air Conditioner. For many people they are the ideal solution.

9-Charging the Battery While In a RV Park:

Once a week you can stay in an RV park to charge your batteries. While you are there you can do your laundry, wash your dishes and take a hot shower. Many offer cable TV and Internet access as well. If you pay $20 a night once a week, that is $1040 per year. You could have paid for a generator and had money left over for that. Of course $20 a week is much easier to come up with than $1,000 cash so maybe it is worth it to you. Whether you are charging your battery at a RV park or with a generator, you will need a battery charger.

Your first thought is that any old automotive battery charger will do, but that isn't correct. Deep cycle batteries are fussy on how they like to be charged. A regular charger will lead to poorly charged batteries and their premature death. What you need is a smart charger. Very often they literally will say "smart" on the package. These are three stage chargers that automatically go through bulk, absorption and trickle, phases. They will charge your battery faster and make them last much longer.

10-Install Solar Panels:

This is the ideal solution but it has several drawbacks. First it is expensive. A single 135 watt panel with controller and wiring will be at least $500-$600. Second, on cloudy or rainy days, during winter, or if you are parked in trees, they deliver less power, maybe not enough to meet your needs. Third, you may not have room for them on your roof.

If you have the room and money and live in an area with good sun they are the best possible way to go. **I love mine and wouldn't be without it!** Having all the power I need, for free, for the rest of my life is just an astounding thing!! But I also have a Honda 2000 generator for times when I run out of power.

DEALING WITH HEAT AND COLD:

One of the questions I hear most often from people who are starting out in vandwelling is, "How do you deal with extreme temperatures like heat in the summer and cold in the winter?" While there are things you can do to make your life more comfortable, the bottom line is that if you live in a van, sometimes you are going to be too hot and other times you are going to be too cold, there just isn't any way around it. Let's take a look at some of the options to be as comfortable as possible:

1-Choose a Temperate Location:

If you have a choice of where you live, try to pick a place with a moderate year-around climate. The best one that I know of is in the rain shadow of Mt Olympus around Port Angeles, Washington, which has great weather year around. Some places along the Pacific coast are moderate year around but can get severe storms in the winter. There are so few places with year-around moderate weather that a better choice is to be a snowbird.

2-Be a Snowbird:

Snowbirds move south in the winter and then north in the summer to avoid temperature extremes. The problem with that is you may have to drive a long way to get to better weather. Much better for the environment and your checkbook is to go up in elevation in the summer, and down in elevation in the winter. For every 1,000 feet of elevation you go up, the temperature drops 3 degrees. For example, the temperature at Orlando, Florida may be 100 degrees, but if you drive 500 miles north to Boone, North Carolina, the temperature will be 80 degrees because it is at 6,000 feet. Or, if it is 100 degrees at Quartzsite, AZ, if you drive 250 miles north to Flagstaff, AZ, the temperature will be 75 degrees because it is at 7,000 feet. And, of course, in the winter it is just the opposite. When it is 30 degrees at Flagstaff, it will be 55 in Quartzsite. If possible, I suggest vandwellers live in the western states because they have a gigantic amount of public land you can live on for free while following mild weather. The southwest is mostly desert land owned by the BLM and is open to free dispersed camping in the winter. There is an equally large amount of National Forest at high elevations you can disperse camp on for free in the summer.

Of course many (maybe most) of us can't leave where we are. We have family, friends or jobs that tie us down to one place. Unfortunately most of those places have hot summers or cold winters, or maybe both. So let's look at how to make our vans as comfortable as we can in the heat and cold.

3-Insulation:

We've already talked about insulating the van, so I'll just go over it again briefly. **First**, within the legal requirements of your home state, tint all the windows as dark as you can. That will keep a lot of heat out in the summer. **Second**, cover the windows with Reflectix which is two heavy sheets of aluminum foil sandwiched over bubble wrap. You can buy it at hardware stores like Home Depot back in the insulation area. **Third** put up a curtain/blanket between the back and driving area of the van: All the glass in the front windows will loose and gain a lot of heat, so both for insulation and privacy you want to hang a blanket between them. The heavier the curtain, the better the insulation. **Fourth**, stop drafts: Moving air will make you feel much colder than the temperature would indicate, so you want to find and close all air gaps (especially around the doors) with weather-stripping and caulk. If you still get a draft, consider duct taping either a Space

Blanket or Reflectix around the back door and Velcro it around the side door. **Fifth**, insulate the roof and walls with Styrofoam.

3-Find Shade in a Park or Forest:

Nothing will cool your van better than parking in the shade. **Parks**: When I lived in a city, it was very hard to find shade. I ended up searching all the city parks until I found some that let me park in the shade. Then I spent all my free time there and I loved it. I could go for walks or swims in the pool. I would take my stove over to a picnic table and cook outside so the van wouldn't get hot. **Forests:** If you aren't tied down to living in a city, then the best thing you can do is spend your summers in local forests because they are drastically cooler than cities. There are two reasons for that: 1)The trees provide wonderful shade, 2) There isn't all that concrete/asphalt absorbing and reflecting heat.

4-Use Ladder Racks and Plywood to Cover the Roof:

Sometimes you just have to park in the sun, like while you are at work or when I am parked in the desert for the winter. I strongly suggest you buy a ladder rack for your van and cover it with plywood. Amazon.com is a good place to buy ladder racks or you may be able to pick up a used pair off craigslist.com. They install easily by clamping to the vans rain gutters.

It's easy to mount the plywood, just bolt four 2x4's to the ladder rack(every two feet) and screw the plywood to them. The sun will quickly damage the plywood, so be sure to paint it with high quality, UV resistant exterior paint (white is best because it reflects heat). My solar panels are bolted to the plywood, avoiding more holes in the roof of the trailer. If you are worried about stealth, carry a ladder on the rack to hide the solar panel.

5-Put up an Awning:

An awning will shade one of your walls and let you sit outside in the shade. You can buy commercial awnings, but they are expensive. A very good choice is an EZ Up type awning, but they are big, take up a lot of space and they are heavy. Those are bad things when you live in a van. I think making your own out of a tarp and PVC tubes is a better choice. I used 1 1/4 inch PVC tubes, a white tarp, and rope to stake it out. I put screws eyes into my plywood roof to attach the tarp to the roof.

6-Create Ventilation with a Vent:

When it's hot, moving air will make you feel much cooler and a vent will give that to you. Nearly all RVs come with roof vents for the simple reason that they are a very cheap way to cool your home. The standard size is 14x14 and they are cheap and simple to install. Cut the hole with a jigsaw, put mastic tape around the bottom of the vent, and screw it into the roof. Finally, put caulk around the perimeter of the vent and on all the screw holes.

There are three problems with roof vents; 1)If you go away and leave it open, and it starts raining, the rain will get inside the van, 2)If you leave it open while you drive, eventually the wind will rip it off, 3)The sun will eventually crack the cover. A solution to all these problems is a vent cover. I open my vents in the summer and never close them until fall. I don't have to worry about rain, wind, driving, or sun damage. I bought the vents, cover and mastic tape from Amazon.com.You can buy vents with a built-in, powered fan to blow air into or out of the van. The most famous and popular is made by Fantastic Fan which has a great reputation of reliability and customer service.

7-Use a Fan:

I think a portable fan is one of the most important things you can buy to be comfortable in the heat. I use a 12 volt fan called the Endless Breeze (available from Amazon.com) that's made by Fantastic Fan. In fact it is the same fan they put in their roof vents, but in a portable housing. It has the huge advantage that you can move it around so that it is blowing directly on you, even when you are driving. It draws about 3 amps of power at 12 volt. But there are many cheaper models available.

8-Air Conditioning:

One question I hear all the time is can you use solar power to operate an air conditioner? I'm sorry to say, the answer is no, it isn't practical. The only good air conditioning option for vandwellers is to buy either a small portable or window air conditioner and use either a generator or shore power to power them. Since I am a snowbird, I don't need air conditioning and don't have direct experience with them, so this is just an overview to get you thinking. You will have to do your own research for more details. The portable ones are easier to install. You just have to rig up a vent to let air out and a hose to let water out.

I've seen three different ways to use window air conditioners. **First**, the most common way to mount one is to remove one of the back windows of the van and cut a piece of plywood to cover the hole. Then you cut a hole in the plywood that the air conditioner mounts into. **Second,** I once saw a guy cut a hole in the side of the van and mount the air conditioner inside the van with a vent cover to cover the hole. **Third,** another way is to cut a piece of plywood to fit inside the passenger window of the van and to mount the window air conditioner in it when you are parked, and take it out when you are ready to drive.

9-Mr. Buddy Propane Heater:

By far the most popular heater for vandwellers is the Mr. Buddy Portable Heater, made by Mr. Buddy. I own one and know lot of other vandwellers that do as well. They come in three sizes, small, medium and large. The medium size (4000-9000 Btu) is almost perfect for a van. My trailer is well insulated so after about 30 minutes I have to turn it off because it gets too hot. But for most non-insulated vans, it should be just about right.

They are cheap, light and easy to start. They work off the little green propane bottles, but I bought an adapter hose and connected it to a 5 gallon propane bottle, which makes it tremendously cheaper to run. I personally don't leave it on at night, but I know several people who do. One friend has a 24 foot Class C RV and he runs his 24 hours a day if it is cold enough. Another friend has a 35 foot 5th wheel and he heats the whole trailer with just the one large Mr. Buddy heater. He also leaves it on 24 hours a day if it needs it. Another option is the catalytic heaters made for camping by Coleman. I know several people who use them and are very pleased.

Some people are concerned about safety with non-vented heaters. But the way I look at it is if they weren't safe, the company would quickly have been sued out of existence. If you carefully follow the instructions in the owner's manual you will be safe. It will tell you exactly how much ventilation you need and what to leave for clearances around the heater. Read those instructions carefully, and if there is anything you don't understand, call the 800 number provided and ask for clarification. Then enjoy your heater with peace of mind and safety.

CONCLUSION:

In this book I've given you a brief overview of what a vandweller is and why you should become one. I've tried to give you the basic steps to get started in vandwelling, and overcome some of the biggest problems you will face. Now the question is, "What are you going to do with all this information?"

For those of you who are being forced into living in a vehicle against your will, it is my deepest hope that your time in it will be made better and more comfortable by having read this book. If it is, I will be very grateful and consider the time and effort put into the book well worth it.

Hopefully some of you will become vandwellers by choice and will find a new way of life that brings you greater peace and joy than you had before. My hope for you is that you will pass on to others the knowledge you've gained and the wonderful way of life you've found.

For every reader of this book I've created a resource to help you in your new life. I have a website full of detailed information about vandwelling; you can find it here:

cheaprvliving.com

I encourage you to contact me directly with your questions and comments at my blog listed above. I will do everything in my power to respond promptly. Be aware that I am often in remote places without cell or data access, so be patient if I am slow to respond. If I take too long, write me again, I won't be annoyed at all. If you have questions, give me as many background details as you can so I can give you my best answer.

Finally, this book and my websites are not a get-rich-quick scheme, I truly love this life and want to educate and inspire others to find it for themselves. To that end my camp is always open to you both winter and summer. Write me and I will give you directions to my location. You are welcome to join me for a day, week, month or season. If I am working as a campground host, my time will be limited but you are still welcome.

I will not die an unlived life.
I will not live in fear
...of falling or catching fire.
I choose to inhabit my days
to allow my living to open me,
to make me less afraid,
...more accessible,
to loosen my heart
...until it becomes a wing,
...a torch, a promise.

—Dawna Markova